The Science of Meditation

Other Books by the Author

Yoga—The Art of Integration
The Nameless Experience
From Mind to Super-Mind
The Call of the Upanishads
The Intuitive Philosophy
The Play of the Infinite
The Dialogue with Death
The Miracle of Descent
The Being and the Becoming
The Eternal Light
The Creative Silence
Seek Out the Way
The Negative Approach
The Search for Freedom
Towards Integration
The New World of Socialism
Can Fate be Changed
Evolution or the Law of Becoming
Psychology: Racial and National
Journey with Death
Fullness of the Void
J. Krishnamurti and the Nameless Experience

The Science of Meditation

ROHIT MEHTA

MOTILAL BANARSIDASS PUBLISHERS
PRIVATE LIMITED • DELHI

First Edition: Delhi, 1978
Reprint: Delhi, 1981, 1987, 1991, 1995, 1997

ISBN: 81-208-0297-7 (Cloth)
ISBN: 81-208-0298-5 (Paper)

Also available at:

MOTILAL BANARSIDASS
41 U.A. Bungalow Road, Jawahar Nagar, Delhi 110 007
8, Mahalaxmi Chamber, Warden Road, Mumbai 400 026
120 Royapettah High Road, Mylapore, Madras 600 004
Sanas Plaza, Subhash Nagar, Pune 411 002
16 St. Mark's Road, Bangalore 560 001
8 Camac Street, Calcutta 700 017
Ashok Rajpath, Patna 800 004
Chowk, Varanasi 221 001

PRINTED IN INDIA
BY JAINENDRA PRAKASH JAIN AT SHRI JAINENDRA PRESS,
A-45 NARAINA, PHASE I, NEW DELHI 110 028
AND PUBLISHED BY NARENDRA PRAKASH JAIN FOR
MOTILAL BANARSIDASS PUBLISHERS PRIVATE LIMITED,
BUNGALOW ROAD, DELHI 110 007

PREFACE

This book is a sequel to my two previous books entitled : *Yoga-The Art of Integration*, and *The Nameless Experience*. In those two books I have discussed the subject of Meditation largely along the lines of philosophy and psychology. In the present book I have treated the subject from a practical standpoint. Here the theme of meditation is discussed in terms of three main constituents, namely, the brain, the habit-mechanism and the mind. I have described these three as the revitalisation of the brain, the modification of habit-mechanism, and the transformation of the mind. I suggest that these three comprise the subject of meditation. They, together, form the wholeness of spiritual life.

It is needless to say that the brain is the only instrument that we have for dealing with physical situations. It is an instrument of adjustment and adaptation. In the present age when the tempo of life has become very fast, the brain has to master the technique of quick adjustment. But the brain as it functions today is much too slow to deal with the fast-moving changes of life. Some scientists tell us that we use only ten per cent of the brain potential at present with the result that the other ninety per cent is very largely inoperative. To deal with the challenges of life, in a fast moving civilization, the full potential of the brain must be made operative. But for this the brain needs a much greater supply of energy.

It is in this context that I have introduced the subject of awakening Kundalini as only thus can the brain get the energy that it needs. But the awakening of Kundalini does not require the following of intricate Hatha Yoga practices. It can be done in a spontaneous way involving no dangers or hazards ; nor does one need the guidance of an expert. The book discusses this spontaneous way of awakening Kundalini, the biological energy which man's bodily mechanism contains.

Today man must explore the meditative way if he is to resolve his many baffling problems of psychological life. The book has no concern whatsoever with the development of psychic and occult powers.

The modification of habit-mechanism and the transformation of the mind deal respectively with the form and the Spirit of man's spiritual life. Thus the brain, the habit and the mind cover the whole field of meditation. I trust, when man today is experiencing disintegration within and disorganisation without, this practical treatment of the subject of meditation will help him to a certain extent in exploring the possibilities of leading a healthy and a creative life in the midst of devastating changes that are taking place all around.

ROHIT MEHTA

CONTENTS

ONE

THE TYRANNY OF THE OPPOSITES

MODERN man is in search of something which he seems to have lost. Curiously enough he does not know what actually he has lost. However, he has a feeling that he misses something in his life without which his existence is devoid of meaning and significance. He has acquired much by way of comfort and possessions due to the progress of science and technology. By any standard of human history he is prosperous compared to which his richest forebears must be regarded as abjectly poor. His comforts and prosperities seem to have no limit, for, one cannot visualise any halt to technological progress. And yet the modern man experiences a strange phenomenon of poverty in the midst of plenty. This indicates a deep hiatus between the subjective and the objective factors of life. There is plenty so far as man's objective conditions of life are concerned. But in the midst of this outer plenty, man is inwardly poor, nay abjectly poor. He tries to fill up inner poverty with outer riches. But it is a frustrating process, for, the possession even of limitless outer riches would fail to reduce the state of inner poverty.

It is this inner void which has rendered outer plenty bereft of meaning and purpose. Of what use are comfort and convenience if they do not give to man peace and happiness ? Not knowing how to remove inner poverty, modern man enters the race of possessing more and more of the outer goods. Never in human history was the gap between the inner and the outer so great as it is today. Neither the traditional God, nor, conventional religion, neither social morality, nor, intellectualized philosophy can bridge this gap.

Life is indeed an eternal flux where everything is moving even as the waters of the fast moving river present a never-ceasing flux. Man sometimes feels that the outer environment moves too fast. He wishes that time would stop awhile. The flow of time however knows no rest or respite. But sometime man feels that time does not seem to be moving sufficiently fast. These fluctuations in the movement of time are but mind's super-impositions on the normal flow of time. Thus Time which is the normal, natural movement of life is made by man into a hurdle and an obstacle through the projections of the mind.

And so Time which can be and is the greatest ally and friend of man has been rendered an enemy through the projections in which the mind of man indulges. Thus the situations created by the flow of Time, whether fast or slow, seem most irksome to man. He wishes that the natural flow of time should synchronise with the psychological flow of time. When this does not happen he feels intensely unhappy. All his efforts to control the natural flow of time appears frustrating. And it is in the flow of time that the process of man's becoming lies. There is no wonder that the entire process of becoming tires and exhausts him, for time seems to move slow when he wants it to go fast, and it seems to go fast when he wants it to slow down! What is man to do faced with the situations created by the movement of time ?

Human mind which has created the fictitious category of psychological time obviously asks man to fight, and fight relentlessly, the situations created by the flow of natural time. Thus does he hope successfully to super-impose on the movement of natural time, the flow of psychological time which can go faster or slower as per the dictates of the mind. But such a struggle is self-defeating, and yet man continues to fight against the situations created by the flow of time. There is no wonder such a struggle dissipates man's energy with the result that he is unable to face the newer and newer challenges posed by Time. When he realizes that struggle against Time is of no avail, he submits to the so-called vagaries of Time, hoping that future would bring happier tidings. But the hoped-for future seems never to come because of the slow movement of Time. And so submission, too, is of no avail, for, it also tires and exhausts him. The waiting for the hoped-for future seems unending. But beyond struggle and submission there is no other way open to the mind of man. To alternate between struggle and submission appears to be a movement in a closed-circle. One may go round and round in this circle for millennia, but one will not be able to step out of mind's prison house even after such a long passage of Time. What then is man to do ? If neither struggle nor submission brings relief from the tyranny of Time, where must he go ? The Mind of man has absolutely no answer. A movement between the two opposite points is the only way which the mind is able to suggest. Here the two opposite points are struggle and submission.

The Eastern Philosophies have given a different word to indicate the flow of Time, and it is Karma. Karma is indeed a movement of Time, from the past to the future. Man desires to have control over this movement of Karma, and it is this which he tries to do by wanting to cover up the movement of natural time through the super imposition of the time-flow created by the mind out of its own background of likes and dislikes, of rejections and indulgencies. But as we have seen, such superimposition is of no avail. It is like hiding one's face in sand, Ostrich-like, hoping that by so doing the existent will be rendered non-existent. Such super-imposition implies a refusal to see WHAT IS. It is out of such a refusal that man engages himself either in struggle or submission. One struggles against what Karma brings, or one submits to its dictates hoping that by so doing the future will bring joy and happiness. The question is : What else can man do ? Beyond struggle and submission is there any other way to deal with the situations of life.

Human mind functions by formulating the two opposites.

What is called the psychological time is nothing but mind's movement between these two points. The two points may have their numerous ramifications, but still they are circumscribed fundamentally by the two opposite points—the alternatives of the mind. And so in the face of any given situation, the mind invariably points to alternatives or opposites. Mind's approach is either or, and so in dealing with the problem of Karma, it can speak of either struggle or submission. Outside the two opposites mind has no existence. It exists only by a movement of continuity between the two opposites. By no process of thought can one step out of the closed circle of the opposites. The opposites may be dressed up in a new manner, or they can be given different names—but still they remain the same so far as the content is concerned. Thought must move within the campus of opposites. This is the inherent limitation so far as the process of thinking is concerned. Thinking can only be in opposites, and the more clearly defined are the opposites, the more definite is the process of thinking. An alert mind is one which can formulate the opposites with reference to any problem or situation in the most precise and definite manner. A dull mind does not see the opposites, but an active mind does. And so the way which an alert mind can indicate for dealing with the challenges of life is the way of the opposites, the way of Struggle or the way of Submission. The mind by its thought process cannot visualise anything else.

But is there a Third Way ? If so, what is it ? If there is no Third Way then man must get reconciled to the state that his problem can never be solved. But surely this cannot be. There must be a Third Way. However, this way cannot be described ; it can only be experienced. It can be discovered, but cannot be defined. If it could be defined then the mind would catch hold of it, and formulate its opposite, which in terms of the mind would be the Fourth way. When this is done then the mind can move between the two newly formulated opposites, and thus once again postpone the solution of life's problems. A movement between the two opposites is indeed a movement of postponement. And mind for ever is interested in postponing a solution, for, only in postponement can mind seek its continuity.

How do we know that there is a Third Way along which life's challenges can be effectively met ? What is the Way to its discovery ? It is quite obvious that the Way to it cannot be found within the precincts of the thought-process. Unless there occurs a break in the continuity of thought, this new way cannot be discovered. This break in continuity may be just for a split-second, or it may be for longer duration. But the break is essential, for, it is only in such a break that an opening in the closed circle of thought can be made.

The discovery of the Third way is possible only in the experience of Meditation. One may call it the discovery of the Third Way, or one may call it the Opening of the Third Eye. There is no difference between the two. It is only in the opening of the Third Eye that the Third Way can be seen. The experience of Meditation does not come within the campus of the Mind. It is outside the realm of thought, even the subtlest and the most abstract thought. But the opening of the Third Eye has nothing to do with the possession of Occult powers, the development of super-physical faculties like clairvoyance. H.P. Blavatsky says in the *Secret Doctrine*, while writing about the Third Eye :

> ......the faculty which manifests through it is no clairvoyance as ordinarily understood i.e. the power of seeing at a distance, but rather the faculty of spiritual intuition, through which direct and certain knowledge is obtainable. This faculty is intimately connected with the 'Third Eye'.

The Third Eye is the Eye of Śiva according to Hindu Mythology. Now the very meaning of the word Śiva is well-being. And so the opening of the Third Eye bestows on man well-being, bliss or happiness. It is in the opening of the Third Eye that man is freed from conflicts. With the opening of the Third Eye all that is ugly and meretricious gets destroyed, and man is rendered inwardly pure. With the opening of this eye it is possible for man to see the Third Way, away from struggle and submission, by treading which he can solve the erstwhile baffling problems of life. Thus the opening of the Third Eye and the Discovery of the Third Way are two sides of the same medallion. Here man is endowed with true spiritual insight which enables him to step out of the closed circle of the mind and see life afresh. The energies that were dissipated in the conflicts created by the mind are regained, for, in the opening of the Third Eye man discovers the secret of renewing energy. On the spiritual path he needs energy, nay, he needs to know the secret of renewing energy. In the experience of Meditation, whenever it occurs, there is the opening of the Third Eye and therefore the discovery of the Third Way.

Modern man is torn asunder by inner psychological conflicts which are the creations of the mind. It is obvious that mind cannot resolve them ; in fact, the more it tries to resolve them, the more complicated they become. And so man must explore a new Way which is not of the mind. The mind must be rendered mind-less, to use the phraseology of Maitrī Upanishad, if man is to free himself from the interminable conflicts in which he is caught. And it is in the state of Meditation that Mind can be rendered Mind-less. Thus meditation has become imperative for the modern man if he is to be free from the tensions, strains and stresses of the technological civilization. He can ignore the way of Meditation only at his own peril. In the closed circle of the Mind, a problem can be shifted, but not resolved. But the psychological crisis that has overtaken humanity is of such an urgent nature that man can no longer afford the luxury of merely shifting the problem, or, of seeking a mere postponement with regard to its resolution. Man must act, and act immediately, for his own psychological survival. For this, he must explore the secrets and mysteries of Meditation. What are these secrets ? And how are they to be unravelled ?

TWO

THE UNCOVERED INTERVAL

IT has been rightly said that Life is Relationship, which implies that to live is to act. Action is an integral part of one's living. We must act with reference to life's situations, to what the flow of Karma brings. But the question is : How to act rightly? Right Action has been defined as doing the right thing, at the right time and in the right manner. This is the *what*, the *when* and the *how* of all actions with reference to the challenges and the impacts of life. It is somewhat easy to understand the Content and the Pattern of Action, but to know the right moment for the performance of action seems extremely difficult. Since time is in a state of constant flux, or, to put it differently Time itself is flux, before one can become aware of a moment, that moment slips into the past. And so the practical question is : How to act at the right moment knowing that one cannot hold that moment for any length of time ? Even if the Content and the Pattern of action are right, the rightness of the moment in the performance of an action seems out of the reach of man. And yet the success of an action depends upon its performance at the right moment. If the psychological moment is missed, an action, however noble and perfect, fails to produce necessary result. How to be aware of the right psychological moment, and, how to act in that moment even when the moment itself does not last ?

It is hardly necessary to point out that Right Moment is the moment of the present, the moment untouched either by the past or by the future. Human mind in its process of thought moves from the past to the future. It is unaware of the present because the present is a timeless moment. Mind has its being only in time, and since the Timeless Moment implies a cessation of Time, to be aware of it requires the cessation of thought. It is a state where the Mind has to come to an experience of Mind-less-ness. Thus an awareness of the present moment implies the death of the mind. And so, any action performed or initiated by the mind is a reaction either from the remembered past or from the anticipated future. The mind for ever is a stranger to Right Action. Its actions arise out of the two opposites of the past and the future. One can act rightly only when the process of thought ceases. This is indeed the state of Meditation, and so, man can act rightly only in the perception that is vouchsafed to him in the state of Meditation. If in meditation there takes place the opening of the Third Eye, then surely this Eye brings the perception of that Moment, the right or the psychological moment in which alone right action is possible. It has to be understood that Right Perception is itself Right Action. What the Third Eye perceives is the Third Way. In perception lies the beginnings of action. In conceptual thinking there is always the point of reaction. In perception, and, there alone, true action is born. If such perception comes in the moment of Meditation then one must know what meditation is, what is its technique, and what does it do whereby the cessation of thought takes place ?

But before we can comprehend what Meditation is, we must be clear as to what Meditation IS NOT. There is much confusion that prevails in the minds of people, both in the East as well as the West, regarding the subject of Meditation. It is due to this confusion that many practices of Meditation, more spurious than genuine, are in vogue today. Modern man's need for meditation is so urgent that he is willing to make any experiment that is suggested in the field of Yoga and Meditation. He has reached the tether of all his mental efforts, and has found, that, while he went out in search of bread, he got stone instead.

One must be clear in one's understanding of the subject of Meditation that it is not a state of unconsciousness or Semi-consciousness where one is completely oblivious of all sense impacts. There is a misconceived idea of Meditation which says that the mind must be completely cut off from all sensorial intimations. In these practices it is very often suggested that the eyes must be closed and the ears too must be plugged so that one neither sees anything nor hears anything. This amounts to rendering the consciousness absolutely insensitive. Surely this is not meditation, for, meditation implies right perception of things. Meditation also does not imply violent processes of breathing and adopting awkward and inconvenient postures of the body.

Sometimes it is suggested that meditation is a repetition of certain MANTRA either given by a guru or taken from some sacred book. It has to be understood that all repetitive processes dull the brain as well as the mind. And this dullness is very often mistaken for silence or quietude.

The dull mind and the silent mind are poles apart, for, while the former is a state of passivity, the latter denotes a condition of negativity or extraordinary sensitivity. In Meditation the mind of man must be rendered sensitive so that it can perceive what IS, and not what the mind has projected or super-imposed.

There is a common misconception about Meditation which says that it is a process of deep and profound thinking, that it is an act of prolonged reflection on some abstruse or abstract subject. One must understand that Meditation is not a process of thinking, for, after all, by any act of thinking, howsoever prolonged and profound it may be, one cannot step out of the closed-circle of the mind. One can think about only what one knows, and so such thinking must keep us confined to the circle of the known. And so the Unknown or the Third Way can never be found by even the most abstruse process of thinking. Thinking will keep us tied within the campus of the opposites, but our fundamental need is to discover a way which transcends the alternatives of the Mind. And so Meditation is not a process of thinking or a process of reflection.

If this be the case, then one would readily state that meditation must be a process of stopping the act of thinking. But meditation is neither thinking nor is it a stoppage of thought. We have noted above that thinking cannot enable us to come out of the closed circle of the mind. But then what about the stoppage of thought ? One has to understand that thought cannot be stopped; not even the strongest will power of man can stop the process of thinking. Thought cannot be stopped by an effort of the mind, no matter how strenuous it is. It is like going to sleep. Surely no conscious effort can bring to man the refreshing experience of sleep. The more the effort to sleep, the farther does one go from the experience of sleep. If meditation is to mean a conscious stoppage of thought then one should resign oneself to constant and frustrating mental effort, with no result whatsoever except tiredness and exhaustion. Meditation is neither thinking, nor, is it a stoppage of thought.

It is generally believed that Meditation requires concentration on a noble and an elevating subject. First of all meditation is not a process of concentration. Such a process is by its very nature exclusive, which implies that certain undesirable and unwanted thoughts should be stopped from coming in. But as no conscious stoppage of thought is possible all processes of concentration are bound to prove self-defeating. Secondly, meditation is not concerned with any particular subject either. Just because the subject is God, or Truth, or Beauty or Goodness or any such noble and elevating concept, one does not thereby come any nearer to meditation. In the ultimate analysis meditation is bereft of all subjects. All subjects have to drop away before one comes to the scintillating experience of meditation. And so it does not matter where and with what subject one begins one's meditation. Even the noblest and the most elevating subject has to go before the experience of meditation arrives.

We have noted above that meditation is not an act of concentration where there must ensue a process of exclusion. All exclusion implies a conscious stoppage of thought or certain type of thoughts. One is apt to believe that if meditation is not an exclusive process of concentration then surely it must be an act of absorption. Needless to say that in absorption there is identification instead of exclusion. Identification is surely another word for indulgence. If exclusion is resistance, absorption is identification. We are once again caught in the opposites of the mind. The opposites of the mind are a married couple; you cannot have the one without having the other too. It is obvious that indulgence must breed resistance even as resistance must take its rise from indulgence. Besides behind absorption there is to be seen the workings of a toy-psychology. There must be something in which one gets absorbed. So long as one can play about with that 'something', so long one is freed from the distracting factors of the mind. This something may be a picture or an image, it may be a *mantra* or a sublime sentence—it does not matter what it is, for, it is a toy which is needed in order to be absorbed even as a child needs a toy with which to play about. Immersed in the toy, the child does not weep; but take the toy away and the child is lost in uncontrollable tantrums. The so-called grown-ups are no better even though their toys may be different. The mind that needs an outer stimulus for being quiet lacks maturity whereas the experience of meditation can come to a mind that is extra-ordinarily mature, and therefore self-sufficient. Meditation is neither resistance nor is it indulgence with regard to any form of thinking. Neither thinking nor the stopping of thought—such is the paradox with which we are confronted as we delve deep into the understanding of Meditation.

What is this state of neither thinking nor stoppage of thought, neither resisting nor indulging, neither excluding nor identifying ? In the ancient and profound book of Kashmir Saivism, entitled *Vijñānabhairava*, there is an instruction given to the student of meditation which says 'Keep attentive between the two breaths'. It further asks the student to understand the state 'where sleep has not yet come, but wakefulness has vanished'. The Mind of man cannot understand the state of being neither asleep nor wakeful. This is not a condition of being half-asleep

-awake. It is a state where there is neither sleep nor ness. Obviously this state speaks of an interval—an interval between two breaths, an interval between two thoughts or between two experiences. The mind of man knows no such interval, for, it always casts a screen of continuity on all that happens. It gives a continuity to otherwise still pictures through the working of its own projecting mechanism. It is this projector which covers up the interval. And so what we see is only continuity but the phenomenon of life is discontinuity in the midst of continuity, intimations of the unmanifest in the midst of manifestation. If we see only the ceaseless movement of manifestation and never comprehend the stillness of the Unmanifest then the movement of manifestation will be bereft of all meaning. It is through the intimations of the Unmanifest that the Manifest becomes significant. But such intimations can be felt or experienced only in the interval of discontinuity. The perception of the Interval comes only to the Third Eye, and it is only in the Interval that the Third Way can be found. In the *Voice of the Silence*, H. P. Blavatsky speks of :

> ......the right perception of existing things, the knowledge of the non-existent.

The Third Eye, the eye of spiritual insight, has the right perception of existing things, and therefore brings to one the knowledge of the non-existent.

It needs to be noted that the Non-existent is not the invisible, for, while the latter has existence on the non-physical planes, the former is the Unmanifest. When one has a right perception of existing things then one realizes that the Unmanifest is indeed the Ground in which the Manifest exists. It is the Unmanifest that sustains the Manifest. All movements of the Manifest, all its processes of Becoming, derive their meaning and significance from the Unmanifest. But the intimations of the Unmanifest arrive in the field of manifestation only in the interval between two movements, between two breaths or between two thoughts. It is in the interval that the Vision of the whole is vouchsafed to man. And Meditation is indeed the Awareness of the Interval. But this is possible only when the continuing projections of the mind cease. When one thought has ceased and the other thought has not begun, there comes into being a Timeless Moment of the Interval. It is truly a Creative Interval, for, here one gets the intimation of the Unmanifest in terms of which the Manifest can find new direction for its movement. The experience of the Interval is verily the experience of Meditation. The Interval cannot be described, nor can it be defined. It is a Timeless Moment which can have no extensions in Time.

But does Meditation only mean an Awareness of the Interval ? What happens after that awareness ? Surely Meditation is not an escape into some Land of Bliss or Nirvāṇa. Man's consciousness cannot always abide in the Timeless Moment. It functions in the field of Time. Does the experience of the Timeless Moment indicate a denial of the Time process ? If so, such meditation has no validity in man's daily life. It can have no relevance in the solving of the baffling problems of life. The man of meditation is not just the ascended he, he is also the descended he. From the Timeless Moment he must return into the field of Time.

But the question is: Will not such descent bring into his life frustration ? Will the field of Time recognise the language of the Timeless Moment ? With what instruments will the man of meditation convey the intimations of the Unmanifest ? Will not such subtle intimations be smothered by the continuous, and sometimes ruthless, activities of the Manifest ? If Meditation is an escape from the actualities of life, then it has no validity. And if meditation does not bring about the total transformation of one's being so as to be able to translate the Intimation of the Timeless into the fields of Time, then it has no relevance whatsoever with the struggles and turmoils of the daily life.

The subject of Meditation must be explored both in breadth as well as depth. In its depth it speaks of the Communion with the Unmanifest — The Non-existent, to use the phrase used by H. P. Blavatsky. But meditation as understood in terms of breadth speaks of the Communication of the Intimations of the

Unmanifest to the entire field of manifestation so that the parched fields of daily life may be irrigated by the fresh waters of the Transcendental and the Timeless experience vouchsafed in that awareness of the Interval which truly is the core of meditation. The man of spirituality has to be both Effective as well as Efficient. His effectiveness depends upon his receiving of the Intimations of the Unmanifest, but his efficiency depends upon his ability to translate those intimations into the language of the work-a-day world.

Modern man must undergo a total transformation in his life if he is to find lasting solutions to the perplexing problems of life. This demands the establishment of a rhythm, an unbroken rhythm, between Communion and Communication, between the Intimations of the Unmanifest, and their translations in the every day life of man. What is this total transformation, and how is man to come to it so that the process of becoming is constantly inspired by the touch of the Being ?

THREE

THE TRIPLE TRANSFORMATION

IT is quite obvious that functioning merely from the plane of the mind one cannot solve the problems created by that mind itself. One has to rise to a higher dimension in order to understand, in proper perspective, the situations operating at the lower dimension. It is only through such perception that one can resolve satisfactorily the problems obtaining at the lower dimensional level. A mere linear movement does not help; there has to be a vertical movement in order to comprehend life's situations in depth. A linear movement denotes an extension of consciousness, along the same dimensional existence. A vertical movement signifies an expansion of consciousness so as to touch a higher dimensional existence. An expansion of consciousness is a movement in depth. Paul Tillich says that modern man has lost one dimension of his existence, and that is the dimension of depth. He further says:

> Modern man seeks depth by cutting into the surface. But the depth is known only when it reveals itself, and ever withdraws from the probing mind.

The probing mind finds that which it has already projected; And it is only when the activities of the probing mind cease that one can comprehend the Depth. To understand anything in depth, thus, requires a total silence in the realm of the probing mind. The silence of the probing mind is indeed the experience of Meditation. It is this which initiates a total transformation of man. This transformation of man has fundamentally two constituents — one, the process of Ascent, and the other, the experience of Descent. Ascent, however steep and rigorous it may be, will not bear fruit in one's spiritual endeavour. There has to be a Descent to bring the spiritual journey to its fulfilment. With Descent there comes into view the new Dimensional perspective. The reaching of the New Dimension is not the result of Ascent, for the process of Ascent is but an act of extension, not of expansion. Spiritual life and the religious life are not identical. The latter constitutes a linear movement while the former denotes a vertical movement, or a dimensional movement. The Bhagavad Gītā, in its Second Discourse, speaks about the vertical or the dimensional movement when it says :

> That which is the night of all beings, for the spiritual man is the time of waking; when other beings are waking, then is it night for the man of spiritual insight.

Such a dimensional change indicates a total transformation in the different layers of man's consciousness. Spiritual life is not a life of mere modification, it signifies a psychological mutation where all parts of one's being undergo a total change. Meditation which is the door to spiritual insight demands this total transformation. It is in the background of such transformation that the exhilarating experience of Meditation arrives. Psychologically speaking this transformation is both at the conscious as well as the sub-conscious levels. Not only that, the transformation is such that one's consciousness opens out to the direct impact from the Unconscious, or, better still, the Universal Unconscious. The Buddhists call it the *Ālaya* H. P. Blavatsky says in *The Voice of the Silence:*

> Behold how like the moon, reflected in the tranquil waves, Ālaya is reflected by the small and by the great, is mirrored in the tiniest atoms, yet fails to reach the heart of all. Alas

> that so few men should profit by the gift, the priceless boon of learning truth....

To open out one's consciousness to this priceless boon of learning truth, is to receive the benediction from above. This indeed is the Descent, but the experience of Descent comes when one has dissolved the subconscious or the personal unconscious, for, so long as the personal unconscious subsists, so long the touch with the Universal Unconscious cannot be established. Meditation demands a total transformation of the threefold nature, namely, of the Conscious, the Sub-conscious and the Unconscious. The change at the Conscious level indicates the establishment of a direct relationship with the Unconscious so that the door between the Conscious and the Unconscious is flung open facilitating an easy passage between the two. As stated above the Triple Transformation is *sine qua non* for real Meditation.

Patañjali in his Yoga Sūtras speaks of the triple transformation of the mind in the context of *Dhāraṇā-Dhyāna-Samādhi* which according to him have to be taken together.

H. P. Blavatsky in her *Voice of the Silence* also speaks of the threefold transformation. She says therein :

> Three Halls, O Weary pilgrim, lead to the end of toils. Three Halls, O conqueror of Mara, will bring thee through three states into the fourth and...thence to the worlds of Rest Eternal.

The simile of the Three Halls used by H. P. Blavatsky describes the self-same threefold transformation about which we have stated above. Sri Aurobindo in his *Letters on Yoga* speaks of the triple transformation of the physical, the vital and the mental. What does this threefold transformation mean in terms of one's daily life ? If the experience of Meditation comes only in the wake of this triple transformation then we must know what one needs to do in one's every-day life so as to come to it where alone the Third way can be found, the Way, by treading which, man can come to the lasting solution of the baffling problems of life ?

In any act of Meditation three factors are involved. One, the Brain and its functioning; two, the Behaviour-patterns and the functioning of habit-mechanism; and three, the Mind and its quality. The threefold transformation demands that there must be change in the functioning of the Brain, in the functioning of the Habit-mechanism, and in the functioning of the Mind.

It must be noted clearly that mind and Brain are not identical. There is still a controversy going on in scientific and psychological circles as to whether they are identical; and if they are not, how are they related to each other ? There have been many theories like Epiphenomenon and Parallelism into which we need not go. Suffice it to say that modern researches in Para-psychology, both in *psi* as well as *pki* phenomena, have indicated that Mind and Brain are different even though related one to the other. If one may use a simile, the Mind may be compared to a radio-station, and the Brain to a radio-set. The radio-station functions on many frequencies, and it is quite possible that the particular radio-set is unable to pick up all programmes transmitted along all the wave-lengths. Just because a radio-set is not able to pick up a particular wave-length does not mean that no transmission is going on along that particular frequency. The human Brain, as it is constituted today, may be missing many of the transmissions sent out by the radio station which the Human Mind is. Professor Penfield, who is a great authority on Human Brain, while agreeing that there are many demonstrable mechanisms in the brain which work quite mechanically when called upon to act, asks:

> But what is the agency which calls upon these mechanisms, choosing one rather than another? Is it another mechanism or is there in the mind something of different essence ?...In conclusion it must be said that there is as yet no scientific proof that the brain can control the mind or fully explain the mind. The assumptions of the materialists have never been substantiated.

The above statement by one who is an authority on the subject of the human brain indicates that there needs to be postulated the existence of some entity which has the power to set in motion one cerebral mechanism in preference to another such mechanism as a more suitable device to meet the requirements of an incoming stimulus or a challenge posed by life. We live in an age of computer-mechanics where remarkable computers have been produced which solve intricate problems in a matter of a few seconds or minutes. While this is true, there has been no goal-setting computer yet envolved. The computer has to be given a goal or a direction, and when this is done it can move with remarkable speed to produce the result. The brain no doubt acts like a computer, but it has to be fed properly. Not only that, it has to be given a goal or a direction in which to move. In order to understand the goal-setting and the problem-solving mechanism, we must examine the functioning both of the Mind and the Brain. This is essential if we are to lay a proper foundation for the raising of the stupendous structure of Meditation.

It is said that while the Brain is like a computer there is no computer which is like the brain. The mechanism of the brain is most amazing. It has remarkable intelligence to deal with varying situations of life. It looks after the needs of the body in a manner difficult to understand. John Pfeiffer says in his book *Human Brain*:

> ... sugar is one of the body's energy-building substances and we must have just the right amount, no more and no less. We walk a biological tightrope between coma and convulsion, the possible results of relatively slight changes in blood sugar levels. But the brain usually receives advance notice of impending trouble. It receives a steady flow of information about current sugar levels, and makes adjustments as effectively as a pilot guiding an aeroplane through a storm. If there is too much sugar, the excess is burnt up and excreted. If there is too little, the liver is instructed to release the proper amount of reserve sugar. Notice what such control implies. The brain must know the desired sugar level, about a sixtieth of an ounce for every pint of blood, on the average. It must go by

similar standards in regulating breathing (most of us inhale and exhale eighteen to twenty times a minute) and heartbeat rates (about seventy times a minute) and in holding body temperature at 98.4 degrees Fahrenheit.

One can quote many such instances denoting the remarkable ingenuity of the human brain in dealing with the proper regulation of bodily needs. The biological well-being of the body is perfectly safe in the hands of this remarkable instrument built by Nature, namely, the Human Brain.

We have to remember that the Human Brain has two components, one, the Old Brain and the other, the New Brain. The Old Brain is our legacy from animal existence, or may be, even prior to it. But there is the New Brain, the cortex, which is the result of human evolution. It belongs entirely to humanity, and is therefore comparatively young. It is a growing organ since humanity is still in its infant, or only post-infant stage in terms of the evolutionary process. Brain forms a very important part in the whole evolutionary story. Evolution as studied by science tells us that it is brain which has been a determining factor in the game of survival. Evolutionary history tells us that there was a time when the earth was lorded by huge and massive creatures like the Dinosaurs. There was a period in nature's history when these giants moved about as if the earth was meant only for them. And yet when we open the next chapter of Evolutionary history we find that these giant creatures have disappeared and their places have been taken by tiny creatures whose existence was not even noted by those giant animals. What was the secret of this strange replacement of the giants by creatures so small and tiny? The secret is to be found in the fact that while the former had brains with very limited adaptability, the latter had brains with greater power of adjustment. And in the struggle for survival, those with greater brain capacity continued to exist while those with lesser brain capacity were wiped off. They lost the game of survival. Thus the role of brain is such that it exercises a determining influence on the trends of evolutionary movement. Those with small brains had a limited range of adaptation. So long as changes, geological and otherwise were slow on the face of the earth, the question of wider and changing adaptation did not arise. When the earth conditions were comparatively static, the creatures who had survived thus far could continue even with the limited brain-capacity. But when the earth-changes became rapid, the game of survival became more and more fierce. These changes necessitated quicker and wider capacities of adjustment and adaptation. This implied development of greater capacities of the brain, for, brain is the only instrument of adaptation to outer conditions of life. During certain turning points in evolutionary history, the need for a newer adaptation always arose. It is during such turning points and geological crises, that greater power of brain-adaptation became necessary. In the struggle for existence, it was the greater brain power that assured survival. And so the brain did exercise a powerful influence in the evolutionary struggle. Man succeeded against the beast because of this greater power of the brain. In muscular strength man was feeble compared to the strong and powerful animals of the forest. But the greater brain power of man enabled him to succeed in the game of adaptation. Man possesses a brain whose powers are most astonishing, and yet the New Brain is only an infant, capable of un-ending growth in its powers of adjustment and adaptation.

It is an established fact that there is a close relationship between the Mind and the Body. The prevalence of Psychosomatic diseases has proved that Mind and Body are closely linked one to the other. It is not merely that the Mind affects the body, but it is also a fact that the Body affects the Mind. Even in traditional religious disciplines the aspirant is asked to be careful about his food, for, food seems to affect the condition of the mind. It is believed that hot and stimulating food excites the mind so that it is not able to pursue its deep reflective activities. A man of meditation is asked to refrain from certain types of food and drink. This shows that there is an inter-relationship between the Mind and the Body. It is not merely the body that affects the Mind, it is also the other way — the Mind affecting the Body.

The mind soaring high into metaphysical or aesthetic or mathematical realms cannot but affect the Brain also while it is engaged in those activities. If the Brain is not affected then the adventures of the mind are bound to prove sterile, for, there will be no corresponding effect on one's physical actions and behaviour. A spiritual experience must needs reflect itself in bodily patterns and actions. And so Mind and Body must function together for healthy intellectual and spiritual life. If the mind is active and the brain unresponsive and passive then one is bound to feel frustrated. Similarly if the Brain is very active but the mind lost in the inertia of the past then that would also bring into existence an unhealthy state. The Mind and Brain must meet at the same level, at the same time and with the same intensity if one is to lead a healthy and creative life.

Unfortunately in spiritual treatises, both ancient and modern, sufficient attention has not been given to the problem of the Brain. It has been presumed that in spiritual and Yogic matters, brain does not count for anything. And so it can be ignored in all serious spiritual disciplines. Nothing can be further from truth. In all spiritual adventures both the Mind and the Brain must be fully involved. It is not enough that one is concerned merely with changing the quality of the Mind, one has also to consider the capacity of the Brain to translate the great achievements of the Mind at the level of behaviour-patterns and bodily activities.

We have seen in the story of evolution, that during periods of physical crises, the units of life that possessed greater brain capacity were able to survive, while others, however strong and mighty in bodily structure, were wiped away. Thus Brain is a principal factor in the struggle for biological survival. At the level of man it is not just the biological survival that matters. There is also the problem of psychological survival. But these two cannot be separated, as psychological survival requires a strong biological base. The question of psychological survival would become meaningless if there be no biological survival. It is a psycho-somatic phenomenon.

Man is witnessing today an unprecedented crisis where both

the psychological as well as biological survival are at stake. And so it is of the highest importance that a serious attention be paid to the problem both of the Mind as well as of the Brain, for, both must function in a manner whereby they can deal effectively with the new challenges of life. Pandit Gopi Krishna in his book, *Kuṇḍalini — The Evolutionary Energy in Man* says :

> It is a great mistake to treat man as a completely finished and hermetically sealed product, entirely debarred from passing beyond the limits imposed by his mental constitution. There is a big gap between him and the most intelligent anthropoid apes. whose habits, it is said, he shared only a few thousand centuries ago, advancing in an inexplicable way beyond the mental boundaries reached by the members of that family.

The human situation today is such that a new species of man must be born if the present crisis of consciousness is to be resolved. The new species of man of course will be fundamentally psychological. But a psychological species cannot come into being without an appropriate change at the level of the human brain. The activities of the Mind and the Brain must synchronise, for, the new psychological species of man must also function at the physical and the biological level. If the biological mechanism falls short of the psychological mechanism then a new and a more fierce conflict is bound to arise. And one hears the rumblings of such a conflict already in the present-day-civilization.

We must enquire as to the nature of the new biological mechanism before we seriously consider the changes in the mental mechanism, for, in order to go far one must begin near. And surely the Human Brain is the nearest point from where one can begin the stupendous journey to scale the spiritual Everest of one's life. But before we can consider the question of the new biological mechanism, we must clearly comprehend the role and the functions of the Human Brain with reference to one's spiritual journey.

FOUR

THE RICKETY BRIDGE

THE Human Brain has a number of functions to discharge. It is busy all through the day and the night. It receives constantly, every second, numerous reports from the five senses. It issues instructions to the various parts of the body as per their needs. It has to act in a special manner during biological emergencies. It has to process all the sense-reports and transform them into percepts. One of its principal functions is to serve as bridge between the Body and the Mind. On this bridge goes on continuously a two-way traffic. The Brain transmits information to the Mind in the form of percepts formed out of the numerous sensations. A percept is made out of the co-ordination of sensations. On the bridge of the Brain also arrive instructions and messages from the Mind. It is a bridge used far more than any other bridge in the world. Such are the varied functions of the Brain which it discharges with remarkable efficiency.

We are told that every second the body's sense organs receive more than ten million sensations. They are not all sent to the brain for processing. Most of them are dealt with by the sense organs themselves. They act like secretaries and deputy secretaries in a vast secretariat. Only about a hundred sense reports per second reach the brain for its attention. These, the brain processes, and sends instructions to various body organs for suitable action. Quite a large number of these major issues received by the Brain are also transmitted to the mind for its information and necessary action. The secretariat of the Human Brain is perhaps the busiest such organisation, nowhere to be found on earth, not even in big states or even in the offices of the big powers.

For the purposes of our studies in Meditation, the Human Brain functioning as a bridge interests us the most. It is this function which is most relevant to the understanding of problems concerning Yoga and Meditation. We will therefore not enter into the marvels of the Brain even though that subject is intensely fascinating. If the Human brain is a bridge between the Mind and the Body, what is the nature of the bridge ? What is its capacity, and is it necessary to strengthen it, taking into consideration the traffic that passes over it ?

It is our common experience that there always remains a gulf between our ideals and actions, between our conceptual aspirations and our behaviour patterns. What we believe is generally not reflected in our behaviour. There is a wide gulf, a deep hiatus, between the flights of the mind and the responses of the body. There are a number of factors involved in this phenomenon — but one of the major factors is, the inability of the Bridge, that connects the mind with the Body, to carry this heavy traffic emanating from the Mind. The bridge is much too weak to bear this load. Needless to say that the Bridge is the Human Brain. And so unless the Bridge is considerably strengthened the gulf between Belief and Behaviour will remain, causing frustrations and dejections in our spiritual pursuits. What has caused this inability of the Bridge to carry the heavy traffic, and how is the Bridge to be strengthened ?

This demands a clear understanding of the state of our brain and the way it functions. It has been noted by scientific investigation that we use only a small part of our brain. Bruce Bliven says, while writing about the unrealized powers of the brain, that "people in general employ only ten to twelve per cent of the capabilities of their brains". This means that nearly ninety per cent of the brain is unused. No wonder, this constant disuse has rendered those parts of the brain atrophied, if not paralysed. We live in a very small world, for, much of the world is shut off from our ken due to the inability of the Brain to respond. We fail to see and hear the subtle nuances of nature and life. Our present capacity of the Brain was developed when outer conditions were not in such fast movement as they are today. Life was comparatively slow, and so the brain as it is functioning today, was able to deal with the situations which operated then. But today life is moving at a terrific speed, the tempo of outer conditions has increased a thousandfold, if not more. It is obvious that the Brain capacity of the slow period cannot meet the challenges of the fast moving civilizations of today.

It is true that it is the Mind that meets the challenges of life, particularly those of a psychological nature. But then the responses of the Mind must be translated at the physical level, for, we live on the physical plane and have to act on that plane. The problems of human relationship, even if they emanate at the mental level, have to be settled in terms of actions and behaviour-patterns on the physical plane. Whether the decisions of the mind are right or wrong, they must be translated at the level of physical actions. And since all physical actions have their source in the brain, it is of imperative necessity to strengthen the brain-potential so that it can respond to subtlest of the mind-impacts, and, translate them in terms of appropriate bodily actions

As we have stated : the brain capacity which was adequate during the earlier periods does not seem to be so in the present age of a fast moving tempo where changes are taking place so rapidly that unless the brain can initiate quick responses of adaptation, there are bound to arise feelings of frustration and desperation. And these are already visible in the life of the modern man. The great unrest that we see everywhere and in all departments of life is a clear indication of this feeling of frustration. The frustration is partly psychological because the mind is unable to come to right choice, and also partly due to the brain's failure to translate whatever decisions the mind may have arrived at. In short the bridge which is constituted by the Human Brain is extremely weak compared to the load it is required to carry.

The difficulty that stands in the way of effectively dealing with the problem of the Brain arises due to two factors. One, the attitude of the so-called scientifically minded people who do not make a distinction between the Mind and the Brain and so treat them as identical. But the second factor is that the so-called spiritually inclined people underestimate the role of the Brain, and, therefore, turn no serious attention to it. Franz Winkler, in his book : *Man : The Bridge Between Two Worlds*, explains the problem of Mind-Brain relationship admirably in the following words :

> The polarity between an outer object and its mental reflection is mirrored in the polarity between the physiology of our brain and the psychology of our mind. The brain itself may well be considered the greatest of all wonders on earth. For its structure bears the most perfect imprint of creative thought on created matter. No wonder that many a scientist mistakes the instrument for the performer, and considers thoughts a product of the brain, as if they were hormones produced by a gland. This is, of course, absurd, because a hormone, like every other product of substance, has natural properties such as physical and chemical qualities, of which thoughts are entirely devoid. Thinking is no more a product of the brain than music is a product of a piano. Nevertheless, the physical properties of the instrument will, to a great extent, determine the quality of the music which is played on it.

While the Brain is the musical instrument, it is the Mind which is the performer of the music. Whether the performer is well-versed in music or not or whether the performer's music has a rich uqality or not will be considered when we come to the transformation of the quality of the mind itself. This will form part of Meditation in its third phase of transformation, the two others being the transformation of the Brain and the transformation of the reactive mechanism of habit. In our present discussion we are concerned not with the performer of music but with the instrument of music. As the above passage indicates—"the physical properties of the instrument will, to a great extent, determine the quality of music which is played on it." And so we must examine the physical properties of the Brain which is the instrument on which music is sought to be played. However divine the performer of music may be, if the physical properties of the instrument are below the mark, then the music played upon it will be too ordinary, not possessing the quality of elevating and uplifting the listeners.

We have seen that the Human Brain, as it is constituted today, is much too feeble to deal with the situations in which it is required to act. It has a small range of adaptation and adjustment. But life is presenting man today with such situations as lie outside the adaptability of the brain as it functions today. With nearly ninety per cent of the brain capacity out of use, we are greatly handicapped in the game of survival, both biological as well as psychological. We have to have brains whose adaptation capacity should have no limit. Not only that, its quality of response with regard to life's challenges must be of the highest order. If the Brain is unable to initiate quick adaptation to the fast changing conditions then our life's experiences will remain incomplete. Such a brain will not be able to establish meaningful relationship with the Mind engaged in dealing with newer and newer psychological challenges with which it is confronted. But the question is: Can the capacity of the Human Brain be increased, and, that too, voluntarily ? We have known about the development of the Brain through outer impacts in the course of evolutionary movement. But to wait for the outer impacts to change the range and the quality of the Brain would be suicidal, for, nature will take a long time to effect the necessary changes. It is the prerogative of man to expedite the evolutionary process. It is within the power of man to initiate new evolutionary movement. Conscious evolution is within the power of man. And conscious evolution must imply a fundamental transformation both of the Mind and the Brain. This is a part of the process of real Yoga. Annie Besant says at one place that 'Yoga is evolution crushed in the palm of the hand'. If that be so the initiative for change must be taken by man himself and not left to the exigencies of outer circumstance. Since Brain is an important link in the chain of conscious evolution, it may be asked pertinently : Can the range and quality of the Brain be changed? If so, how ?

There are many misconceptions regarding the brain and its functioning in the general thinking of most people. We usually speak of the 'brain fag', meaning the brain gets tired. But the fact of the matter is that it does not get tired. The brain is not like a muscle. Its operations are not muscular but electro-chemical in nature. Bruce Bliven says :

> When your brain appears tired after hours of mental work, the fatigue is almost certainly located in other parts of the body, your eyes or the muscles of your neck and back. The brain itself can go on almost indefinitely.

What we generally call as brain-fag is only boredom. And we do get bored in things in which we are not primarily interested. In things of intrinsic interest, the brain can go on without any feeling of tiredness, and that too for any length of time. Brain-experts tell us that the "brain's capacity is almost inexhaustible." To evoke this capacity there is no need to have a larger brain. The brain has twelve-thousand million cells. If they are fully used the capacity of the brain can be increased enormously. To do this requires establishing new centres of learning. At present our learning-centres in the brain are very limited. Our brain-activity moves on in certain grooves; our contact with life is at very few points. Added to this, modern man has moved on towards specialization to such an extent that he can touch life at still fewer points, leaving the large area of life completely out of his ken. This specialization has made us lop-sided in our capacity to meet challenges and impacts of life. In one part of our brain we are mature due to specialization, but in other parts of our brain we have remained immature. There is no all-round development of our brain capacity. But this has become all the more necessary today in the extremely specialized civilization which science and technology have created. Along with specialization we need in man a capacity to respond to numerous impacts from life, for, thus only can his life become rich and free from frustrations.

Brain scientists tell us that in matters of learning, age is no barrier, for, the brain can establish new centres of learning almost at any age, even at the age of ninety. Learning is concerned with an ability to create new reverberating electric circuits in the brain, and the functioning of this process has nothing to do with one's age. The common saying 'I am too old to learn' has no validity so far as the increase in brain capacity is concerned. One can never be too old to learn. It may be that there may happen some slight impairment in the functioning of the brain in old age, but this can be easily corrected so that even old people can go on learning new arts and crafts. The question is not: Whether brain can learn new things even in old age: the question, however, is : How to establish new centres of learning in the brain? This has no relevance to age. Sometimes even young people stop learning and are satisfied with meeting life from only those centres that are active in the human brain. How to learn is the fundamental question not only with regard to Brain, but with regard to leading a full life so that one does not carry on a mere cramped existence, as is the case with us today.

The establishment of new centres of learning in the brain implies bringing into operation the unused potential of this remarkable instrument which man possesses. As we have seen, nearly ninety per cent of brain is unused at present. If the full potential of the brain is brought under operation then we will begin to live in a larger world of which at present we are not conscious at all. The Brain will be able to establish ever-increasing points of contact with life.

The Human brain receives impacts from two sides, from the senses and from the Mind. At present the senses are unable to send full reports to the Brain because the absorption capacity of the Brain is very limited. This limited capacity for absorption has rendered our senses insensitive. Similarly, to the brain come impacts from the Mind, but because the bridge constituted by the Brain is weak it is unable to take the full load which the mind may want to send. The bridge is weak because it has few centres of response, it has a small area under use; the very large field of the brain is otherwise unploughed and untilled. And so this large portion being sterile cannot receive the load that may come from the mind over the bridge. We really live in a very small world both physically and mentally. When mind's instructions to the Brain remain unattended then the Mind too becomes dull, it gets frustrated in its efforts to soar higher and higher in fields of mental achievement. It may carry on its specialised activities but it is not inclined to plough larger areas of the mental field. Thus the weakness of the bridge renders the senses insensitive on the one hand, and renders the mind dull on the other. We are constrained to live very mediocre lives whereas with the activisation of the unused portions of the Brain we could bring newer dimensions to our living.

How is the full potential of the Brain to be brought into operation. This means a change both in the range as well as in the quality of the functioning of the Brain. At present the lower or the animal brain is much larger and virile than the new or the upper brain. This has resulted in a great deal of unbalancing between the two portions of the Brain. With the New Brain greatly activised in range and quality a proper balance will be established between the Animal and the Human parts of the Brain. The Cortex or the Upper Brain is engaged mostly in intellectual growth, but this intellectual development has no chance to survive due to the pressure of instincts coming from the Animal Brain. We cannot rule out the animal heredity; what we must be concerned about is to see that the two parts work harmoniously so that the animal energy is canalised into finer channels supplied by the Upper Brain. The refinement of the animal energy will become easier if the full potential of the Upper Brain is brought into operation.

The late Sir Charles Sherrington, who was a great authority on the Human Brain, while stating that the evolution of the human brain is still continuing, said "Nor is the brain's present state, we may suppose, more than an interim phase, on the way to something else, something better, we may hope." And so according to this authority on Brain, our present state of Human Brain is just an interim phase, not a final one, which means that this intricate organ is in the process of growth. If so, a question arises: Can its growth be expedited? Can we speed up the process of Nature so that the human brain is able to function at its full potential, or near full potential?

We have seen that during all turning points in evolutionary history, it was the brain that determined the problem of survival. A sudden change from Dinosaurs to the sovereignty of small creatures in the evolutionary game denotes a turning point. From animal to man is also a major turning point in evolutionary history. During this transition it was the brain of the human being that gave him superiority over the animals who were strong and mighty in physical structure. Today we stand at another major turning point of history. Sri Aurobindo describes man as a Transitional Being. This means he is on the move to reaching greater heights of being. Today we are witnessing a crisis of consciousness or a crisis of values. Man is on the threshold of a new dimensional existence. Thinkers and Philosophers of the East and the West speak today of the limitations of the mind and are indicating a way beyond the Mind if man is to solve the perplexing psychological problems of his life. This movement beyond the mind will change the very quality of one's being. But if the experiences beyond the mind are to be translated in terms of new behaviour-patterns and qualitatively different actions at the physical level then surely the present brain, functioning at a low potential will be a very inadequate instrument. The bridge connecting the mind with the body will break down again and again, in fact, it will be impossible for it to carry the new category of load sent by the New Consciousness to which man seems to be moving. Yoga has become a prestigious proposition for the modern man because he wishes to reach a different dimensional living where alone he can hope to settle his baffling problems of life. But if this movement in terms of Yoga is not associated with a similar movement for the increasing of the brain potential then the successes in the field of Yoga will lead man to greater and greater frustration due to his inability to translate psychological experiences in terms of appropriate behaviour-patterns at the physical level.

To increase the brain potential, to activise the large unused areas of the brain — this has become the urgent need of man if he is to travel successfully into the New Land of Yoga. How is man to initiate the necessary steps for transforming the Brain so that it is able to work at its full potential?

FIVE

AWARENESS WITHOUT ATTENTION

AS early as the first decade of this century, Sir J. C. Bose, the eminent Indian scientist, made certain startling discoveries as a result of his experiments. He stated that metals, and what we call inert matter, do respond to human feelings of love and hate. He also said that these material objects need from time to time, small periods of rest so as to recover from the stress and strain to which they are subjected in the course of man's use, or mis-use, of them. It is a common experience of many people that razor blades after constant use, get blunt and are not able to give good shaves. But if after use, these blades are given some rest, and then used, one finds that the blades have regained their sharpness during the period of rest. Lyall Watson in his fascinating book *Supernature* says:

> The edge of a razor blade has a crystal structure. Crystals are almost alive, in that they grow by reproducing themselves. When a blade becomes blunted some of the crystals on the edge, where they are only one layer thick, are rubbed off. Theoretically, there is no reason why they should not replace themselves in time.

According to Lyall Watson 'given time', the edges of the razor blade get once again sharpened. Most machines also need this 'time' to recuperate themselves. These machines work better and more efficiently after some time of rest. Now Human Brain is also like a machine. We say like a machine because it is a machine with a difference. The difference lies in the fact that its components, unlike the other machines, are living cells. If machines composed of inert matter need time for rest and recuperation, much more so must be the case with the Human Brain with its living tissues. The Brain gets into a fresh state of efficiency even if there is only a moment of rest, it may be even for a small fragment of time. By itself it does need rest and relaxation, but its relaxation gives to the whole nervous system some time in which to recuperate from the very hard work that they have to do. When the brain rests, the nervous system feels relaxed because there is an easing of tension. After this period of rest, the brain is able to get out of the nervous system greater amount of work, and that too, done with great efficiency.

In modern age man is subjected to a great deal of stress and strain with the result that his nerves are all the time on the edge. We become irritable for no reason whatsoever or for reasons that are utterly flimsy. We experience nervous breakdowns because our nerves have no rest or respite. This is so because there are no moments when the brain has rest and relaxation. Modern man has indeed become a stranger to the art of relaxation. He is all the time highly-strung never knowing a state of nervous calm and quiet. In order to over-power one category of nervous tension he goes to an experience of still greater nervous tension in another field of life. Thus he moves on from excitement to excitement — from the tensions of the home and the office to the tensions of the cinema and the television. In fact, so used has man become to these nervous tensions that he feels bored during such moments when tension is not experienced. He seems to believe that tension is the very core of life. And yet he constantly breaks down under the pressure of these tensions.

It is quite obvious that during the active moments of the Brain our nerves can have no relief, for, they are required to be on attention to discharge the work assigned by the brain. And so if there is to be nervous relief, there must be moments of rest and relaxation for the Brain. Even though the Brain itself is not tired. its efficiency is greatly impaired if the nerves are not in a fit condition. If the nerves cannot discharge their functions well then the brain too becomes fidgety, for, it demands above all an efficient execution of its instructions. In a big office when the subordinates do not work efficiently, the boss himself is upset, unable to give full attention to his own work. This is exactly what happens when the nervous system is overworked and therefore shows forth greater and greater inefficiency in the discharge of its duties.

One of the ways of brain relaxation that we know is Sleep. It is true that during sleep the brain is least active, attending only to certain basic functions. This being the case the nerves also are at rest, not sending fresh impacts to the brain. But the difficulty is: One cannot always resort to the practice of sleep. There are moments during the day when nervous tension mounts up and the brain is unable to work efficiently. Besides, sleep does not always result in the relaxation of the brain. Ordinarily our sleep is much too disturbed by dreams. Very often the dreams are unpleasant and so vivid that one wakes up in the midst of sleep. Dreams of the nightmarish type may be few and far between, but one does get disturbing dreams which break up the moment of sleep. Even otherwise we do not always get up from sleep in a refreshed condition. In fact, we get up very often in the morning already tired and jaded, This may be due to the fact that even though there were dreams we are not in a position to recall them. It is said that ordinarily we dream three times during the night sleep. When we get up these various dreams are mixed up, causing confusion to the brain when we are awake. And so sleep does not seem to solve our problems of nervous tension and therefore of real rest and relaxation for the brain. We will not discuss the question of Dreams at this stage. In a later chapter we will consider the problems posed by dreams. If we could have a totally dreamless sleep, perhaps our problem of brain relaxation, and, therefore, of nervous tension, would be partly solved. Since we ha dly know what a real refreshing sleep is, the avenue of sleep does not seem to be an effective way towards brain rest and relaxation. Besides we require a way of relaxation during our waking hours too when tensions seem to grow and the brain feels heavy and disturbed, unable to discharge its functions efficiently.

There is today a frantic search on the part of the modern man to find release from all types of tension. There are indeed various types of tension. Sometimes it is due to the inability of the mind to find any satisfactory solution to a situation or a problem. The mind is utterly confused and finds no way out. This is psychological tension which we experience very often due to the complexity of the situations in which we find ourselves. We will not discuss this category of tension at this stage. We will take it up when we come to the problems of the mind as distinguished from the problems of the brain. For resolving such psychological tensions one has to go into question of the transformation of the habit mechanism as also of the transformation of the very quality of mind itself.

But there are other tensions dependent upon the functioning of the brain and the nervous system. When the inadequacy of the Brain is unable to receive mind's clear instructions with regard to certain situations then a state of tension arises in one's mind. But it is not of the mind's making — it is because of the low potential in the functioning of the brain. The question of enlarging the active areas of the brain was introduced in the last chapter, and we shall go into the practical aspects of increasing the brain-potential in a later chapter. This is a category of tension from which mind seeks release but cannot find as the cause of the tension is located not in the mind but in the brain. But before we go into the question of intensifying the brain-potential, we have to settle the problem of brain's rest and relaxation. Without such rest, increasing the brain potential will create greater conditions of nervous tension. It would be dangerous to work at increasing the brain potential without clearly understanding the way of quick rest and relaxation of the brain which would give to the nervous system necessary respite in which to recuperate itself.

When the brain is unable to rest or relax then there arise what we have called nervous tensions. Nerves do get tired due to incessant work. It is true that there is nothing like brain-fag, but there is the tiredness of nerves. Nervous and muscular tiredness does arise, and in order to relieve this tension rest and relaxation are necessary. But for this the brain has to rest so that it does not issue fresh orders to the nerves and the muscles. The nervous system may be divided mainly into two divisions — the automatic or involuntary and the voluntary. It is the nerves comprising the voluntary division that need rest. The automatic nervous system has to work on even when we are asleep. But the automatic system has its own checks and counter checks. This system has two sections — the sympathetic and the para-sympathetic. J.D. Ratcliff says:

> The sympathetic system ... stimulates activity and the para-sympathetic ... retards it. If the body were entirely under the control of the sympathetic system, the heart, for example, would race itself to death. If entirely under the para-sympathetic, the heart would stop. The two must be in perfect co-ordination. When quick energy is needed in times of stress, the sympathetic gains the ascendency, speeding up heart and lung activity. In sleep the para-sympathetic lays a calming hand on all bodily activity.

This is so far as the automatic part of the nervous system is concerned. Here there is an automatic device for the rest and relaxation of the nerves. But it is the voluntary part of the nervous system that needs to be brought to periodical rest and relaxation. In this the relaxation of the brain is essential, nay imperative. It is the voluntary system which is active during waking hours and so its relaxation problem cannot be solved completely by the experience of sleep, however refreshing it may be. We need to know how to snatch few moments of relaxation during waking hours. It is not by dozing off or by having 'forty winks' that one can get refreshed.

For the relaxation of the brain, and, for getting relief from tensions, modern man is getting addicted to all types of drugs and tranquillizers, like LSD or Hashish or Marijuana or some such drugs. Today young people in universities are getting dangerously addicted to this practice. These have no doubt tranquillizing effect — but instead of giving relaxation to the brain, they produce a dullness of the brain. A relaxed brain is not a dull brain. A dull brain produces lethargy and indolence so that one is not inclined to act at all. In the soothing effect of tranquillizers one is reduced almost to the state of lotus-eaters. One must see a dog or a cat relaxing. They are completely relaxed, and yet in a moment, if need arises, they jump into activity. There is no time lag between the condition of relaxation and the state of activity. This is so because these animals are relaxed but do not thereby come to a condition of dullness. Drugs and tranquillizers will not solve the problem of tension. In fact when the effect of the drug is over, one is more overpowered by tensions, and has even less vitality to face them.

It is often suggested that by the practice of *Japa* or repetition of mantra one can have brain-relaxation. A mechanical repetition of mantra obviously introduces an element of monotony. The mantra is a sacred word or phrase either given by a guru or taken from some holy book. It is a common experience of most of us that an act of constant mechanical repetition produces its own monotony. And monotony, howsoever produced, creates a dullness of the brain. Even the constant repetition of a mantra must produce this dullness due to the monotony that it brings into being. It is not sufficiently recognised that monotony or repetitive actions produce their own neurosis. There is a new form of nervous tension created by monotonous actions and repetitions. John Pfeiffer says in his book *The Human Brain*:

> ... neurotic disturbances were particularly frequent among men and women who worked on assembly lines and had to go through the same motions over and over again. Repeated tasks, involving the repeated transmission of nerve signals along the same pathways, apparently threw something out of adjustment in the brain. Monotony has long been recognised as a powerful factor in neurosis . . .

One does not often realize the effects of monotony because one is apt to overlook the distinction that exists between the Dullness of the brain and the Relaxation of the brain. A dull brain is passive and therefore prone to avoid all activity. Even after the repetitive process is over the brain will not be inclined to act. One might say that the dullness produced by taking drugs is worse than the dullness induced by repetition whether of a mantra or of anything else. This is true to a certain extent because the drug-taking has its own after-effects along many lines, for, it brings in an element of degeneration in the entire body-system. We find today several meditation practices suggested which replace the drug-taking by repetition of mantras or phrases, whether audibly or inaudibly. It is an act where the nerve signal is being sent continuously along the same pathway. These meditational practices do give a relief, but it is the relief due to dullness and not due to real relaxation. Today in scientific investigations of meditation practices, brain waves are being studied, the alpha, the beta, the theta and the delta waves. And because the slowing down of brain waves is detected it is presumed that the brain has come to a state of relaxation. The testing machine obviously cannot make a distinction between dullness and relaxation, for, the only criterion of judgment it has is the nature of Brain waves. The brain waves can show that the brain activity has slowed down — but the slowing down can mean either dullness or relaxation. And so to determine the state of the brain by the detection of brain-waves is something misleading. In any case, either by drugs or by repetitive activities, audible, or inaudible, all that happens is the dullness of the brain, not a relaxation of the brain. And there is a gulf of difference between the two.

The question is: How can one come to the relaxation of the brain — where the brain is relaxed and yet not dull ? A relaxed brain can spring into activity in no time — but the dull brain cannot. One must clearly understand the secret of brain relaxation before one embarks upon the task of intensifying the brain-potential.

It may be asked : Can one relax consciously ? Is not relaxation through conscious effort a contradiction in terms ? It is true that consciously one cannot relax just as consciously one cannot go to sleep. But one can consciously create such conditions where relaxation can naturally and effortlessly come. It is hardly necessary to point out that any conscious effort to relax would result in increased tension.

It has to be noted that breathing has much to do with the relaxation of brain. Our normal breathing is mostly irregular. This irregular breathing contributes much to the brain-tension. It certainly prevents the creation of conditions in which brain can come naturally to a state of relaxation. If one observes one's own breathing one will realize how irregular it is. It is now fast and now slow, it is now deep and now shallow. There is no consistency in the breathing rate. Now this irregular breathing implies a very irregular supply of energy to the brain. This by itself contributes to brain tension, for, it prevents its efficient working. If daily one could spend some time, five to ten minutes, just observing one's own breathing then in that very observation the breathing will tend to become regular. In Buddhist meditation great emphasis is laid on the observation of one's breathing. In fact, very often it is suggested as a means to the relaxation of brain. In any case the very observation of one's breathing brings about a rhythm so necessary for the regularisation of the breathing-process. The brain needs more and more oxygen for its efficient working. And the only way to supply this oxygen to the brain is by the process of breathing.

Over and above the observation of one's breathing, exercises in deep breathing greatly help in creating a restful state for the brain. Very often our brain gets congested and so feels heavy, or sometime the brain appears to be utterly blank. Both these conditions indicate that the brain is in need of more oxygen. A little experiment in breathing will convince any one that it removes brain's congestion and also supplies greater vitality to the brain. Oxygen is the fuel which the brain needs for its work, and deep breathing certainly is a great source by which this need of the brain is fulfilled.

It is in moments of relaxation that the human brain gets revitalized. This moment of relaxation gives to the nerves their needed rest. And so brain's revitalization brings a feeling of renewal to the whole nervous system. In this revitalization, the most important instrument is *Prāṇāyāma*. In deep breathing and *Prāṇāyāma* there is difference, for, in the latter there is an interval between the inhaling and the exhaling process. In this interval the breath is held within. It is this holding of the breath that gives a large supply of oxygen to the brain. In the normal act of inhaling and exhaling the oxygen that is taken in is immediately expended in the process of exhaling. And so in this, the brain gets very little of its oxygen supply. But in *Prāṇāyāma*, where the breath is held in the interval between inhaling and exhaling, there is good supply of this vitalizing energy in the form of oxygen. One must do simple *Prāṇāyāma*, not complicated as indicated in the book of Haṭha Yoga. In this the breath must be held only as long as one does not feel uncomfortable. The moment discomfort starts, even the slightest, then the held breath must be exhaled. This simple *Kumbhaka* will greatly help in removing brain-congestion and in giving it a feeling of rest and relaxation. As this *Prāṇāyāma* will not need more than ten to fifteen minutes. one can easily snatch this time during waking hours, even when one is engaged in work. It will give that rest to the brain which ordinarily it is not able to get during several hours of sleep.

In the disciplines of Yoga, particularly Haṭha Yoga, spiritual aspirants are asked to take one posture for relaxation and it is : *Śavāsana* which means lying flat on one's back like a corpse. In this the breathing is slowest, and the various parts of the body motionless and limp. This is an excellent way of relaxation. But one may say : How can one lie down during working hours ? It is not necessary to lie flat on one's back, one can sit in a reclined position in a chair or a *dīvān*. In this position while one may be vaguely aware of what is going on, one must make no effort even to observe or listen. One must not make any effort even to observe the thoughts that may pass in one's mind. Let the things and thoughts pass on without observing them. In this reclined position or in the traditional posture of *Śavāasan*, one's brain will get very quickly relaxed.

Modern man gets easily bored. He has to be kept amused and entertained by society. He seems to have lost the capacity for self-entertainment. He is unable to find his own amusement. In such a condition there is no wonder, he gets bored, and that too very soon. Social amusements cannot solve his problem of boredom completely. What is the cause of boredom ? When the brain is occupied for a pretty long time in sending signals to nerves only along one pathway or a limited pathway, then the nerves get tired and the brain gets bored because of the unresponsiveness of the nerves. It is monotony that tires the nerves and the tiredness of the nerves produces a state of boredom for the brain. In the state of boredom no efficient work can be done. It is an indication that rest and relaxation are called for. When bore om comes there must be rest for the nerves that have worked monotonously for a long time, and therefore there must be relaxation for the brain.

It is obvious that when the brain-signals move along the path of the same nerve or the same group of nerves there is tiredness and boredom, impairing the efficiency of the brain. Under such circumstances it is always advisable to break the monotony of the nerves by switching over to some other work for some time. A change of occupation, for however small a duration, helps in breaking the monotony. If one is reading or writing or doing anything for a sufficiently long time so as to create monotony in the nerve region then one can take a break and switch over to something else. One may go and sit idly or walk or pace the room up and down or do little gardening or play with the child or give attention to the dog — or do almost anything. It is not what the new occupation is that matters, it is the breaking of the monotony and that is important. Very often even when a feeling of tiredness comes due to monotony, we try to use what is called our "will power" and concentrate on the work in hand with greater tenacity. We feel it is a weakness of the spirit to switch on to some other work. In such moments it is suggested that one must gird up one's loins and fight the feeling of monotony and boredom.

But this will never help. It will produce greater resistance within oneself, and the nervous mechanism too will resent this action of force or violence. If one switches over for a few minutes to break the monotony then after that small duration one can turn to one's original work with greater energy. The slight break caused by change of occupation gives rest and relaxation both to the brain as well as the nerves. It is said about Sir Winston Churchill that during the second world war when he had to work under great pressures and take momentous decisions, he used to switch over for few moments to painting. He would dab a few colours and continue with his painting as if there was no War and as if he had nothing to do with war operations. After that short diversion into the field of painting or gardening when Sir Winston returned to his war work he felt fresh and energetic enough to take decisions of world importance.

Countless instances can be given from the lives of great men and women of the world who took a few moments off in the midst of their arduous work, and in so doing refreshed themselves so as to pick up their main work with greater fervour and efficiency. Sometimes one may be engaged in writing, doing some creative work, and suddenly the passage between the mind and the brain gets blocked so that the brain is not able to bring through anything. It would be futile at such a time to struggle with the brain and force it to work. Such forced writing would be utterly lifeless. But if one would just take off from the work for a few minutes, do anything that one likes, repair some mechanical gadget or take a stroll and then return to the desk, one will find that once again the passage between the mind and the brain has been cleared, and the brain is able to bring through. There is an effortless flow of ideas. Evidently the brain has been refreshed during those few moments of relaxation. It is not merely sleep that is needed, what is required is a change of occupation for a little while. When this is done the brain and the nerves are able to work once again with great efficiency.

It is said about Mrs. Annie Besant that when working under great pressure she would just switch on for a little while to crime or detective stories and get refreshed to take up her arduous work with greater energy. In 1930, Mahatma Gandhi was preparing for a big struggle against the British Government in the cause of India's political freedom. Those were hectic days when in his ashrama feverish political activities were going on. The Intelligence officers of the British Government wanted to find out as to what Gandhiji was doing at that time in preparation of the struggle. One such officer approached his personal secretary with this inquiry. The secretary told that officer that he could go in to find Gandhiji engaged in learning how to cook a particular delicacy which had taste as well as nutrition value. This great political leader was not concerned about the challenge he had thrown to the mighty British Government and the call that he had sent out to his people to get ready for the struggle. This seemingly ridiculous diversion was to give rest and relaxation to the brain so that it would be ready to handle the task of taking momentous decisions with clarity and efficiency. Thus a little taking off or a change of occupation for a little while relaxes the brain. This is something which any person can do, even the busiest executive and that too during the working hours.

One of the most effective ways of brain-relaxation is to follow the principle of AWARENESS WITHOUT ATTENTION. It means sensorial awareness without cerebral attention. An application of this principle means senses receiving impacts from outside but not sending them to the brain for percept-processing. They remain sensations without being made into percepts. In practical terms it means that if one is listening to music, let the vibrations of music fall on the ear but not transferred to the brain. The brain is required to give no attention to the vibrations received by the organ of hearing. Here the sound vibrations are allowed to fall on the ears without any attention being given as. to what is the nature of music or who sings; one can sit in a chair with or without closing the eyes to find that this pure sensation of hearing creates in a remarkable manner a state of brain-relaxation. One can look at nature and allow the light waves to fall on the retina, but not transferred to the brain for percept-making. This is what we have described as Awareness without

Attention. What applies to hearing and seeing is equally applicable to other senses. One can be aware of the fragrance or taste or touch without any cerebral attention whatsoever. This sensorial awareness without cerebral attention results in brain not sending any instructions to the nerves, nor is the brain sending any messages to the mind. The brain is as it were hibernating — not dull but relaxed. The duration of brain's hibernation cannot be long — it may be for ten to fifteen minutes or may be half-an-hour. But that is enough to refresh the brain and the nerves. One can even go on doing other things, and allow the vibrations to fall on different senses. The moment attention is given to these sensations, the brain will spring into activity and start giving instructions to the nerves. This state of hibernation does not mean that the brain is not attending to its basic functions for which the sympathetic nervous system has to be active. It only means that the voluntary nervous system will be for the time being quiet. One can easily try this experiment of Awareness without Attention for few minutes each day even during working hours. In the beginning a little effort may be necessary as the brain is likely to rush in with its act of recognition. This is an experiment of Awareness without Recognition, for, the attention of the brain results in recognising a particular sensation or a group of sensations. We are not referring to the process of identification when mind enters the picture. Prior to mind's identification there is the recognition by the brain. This recognition comes by the formation of a percept by the brain out of the raw sensations received from the various sense organs. To keep the sensations raw, that is without being formulated into percepts, is what we have termed Awareness without Attention. In the child's life sensations remain raw in the initial stages before they get themselves grouped round the person of the mother. One can come to the freshness of the child state if one could have pure sensations, and not allow them to become percepts. Just to allow the vibrations of sound and light, of taste and touch and smell to fall on sense organ without bringing in the attention of the brain is a very refreshing experience. In a few moments the brain gets relaxed and the nervous tension released.

One can employ all the methods indicated in this chapter for brain's relaxation. It includes *Prāṇāyāma*, restful posture, change of occupation and awareness without attention. One may evolve other methods for relaxation. But it must be remembered that these are not conscious ways of relaxing. They are conscious efforts to create such conditions where the brain and the nerves can come to a natural and an effortless state of relaxation.

Relaxation is a condition prior to increasing the brain potential. In our daily life, particularly when it is subjected to strain and stress, there is great need to have a few moments, from time to time, of rest and relaxation. As one cannot go to sleep again and again, it is necessary to make such conscious efforts as would be conducive to relaxing the brain and bringing rest and respite to the voluntary nervous system. He who does not know how to relax has no right to invoke greater powers for the Brain. With the increase in the brain potential, the need for relaxation will be all the more. The experience of relaxation is an act of withdrawal. One cannot remain in this state of withdrawal all the time. One must return to the challenges of life. What indeed is the way of return so that one can meet the challenges of life effectively ? For this we must explore the subject of increasing Brain's potential.

SIX

THE RELEASE OF ENERGY

MODERN Science speaks of Matter and Energy being interchangeable. Energy in its static condition is Matter; and Matter in its dynamic state is Energy. The words Potential and Kinetic energy give us an indication of the inter-changeability of Matter and Energy. As one Scientist has said 'Energy cannot be created without the destruction of matter, and energy cannot be destroyed without the creation of matter." The whole universe is permeated with energy, vibrating at different levels. In fact, the whole universe can be comprehended only in terms of vibrations. It is energy vibrating at different levels that gives birth to different states of matter, not only the three physical states of matter, but even the non-physical states of matter. Movement from one state of matter to the other is only a change in the vibrational rate of energy. What we call hard matter is only energy vibrating at a particular level. It is the change of matter into energy that has brought us to the wonders and dangers of the Atomic Age. Perhaps Einstein would not have thought that his simple equation would result in the creation of an atom bomb, destroying thousands of people, and maiming many more, in the tragedy of Hiroshima and Nagasaki.

Modern science speaks of various categories of energy such as : Chemical, Thermal, Mechanical, Electrical, Radiant, Nuclear, Thermo-nuclear etc. One might say that all these categories of energy are but expressions of one energy, namely, Cosmic Energy. It is this which permeates the entire universe and expresses itself at different levels. It is to the different expressional levels that differing nomenclature for the same Energy is given, even as *Prāṇa* or Vital Breath is one, but it has differing names according to its functional areas in the Physical Body. From the Nose to the Heart is *Prāṇa* ; from the Heart to the Navel is *Samāna*; from the Navel downwards is *Apāna*; from the Nose to the Head is *Udāna*, and the *Prāṇa* that pervades the whole body is *Vyāna*. It is to the same Vital Breath that these different names are given in terms of the bodily area in which it functions. The same is the case with regard to Energy. It is the same Cosmic Energy which is called by differing names on the basis of its expressional differentiation. Over and above the various categories of energy which we have enumerated above, there is Biological energy too. It functions within the physical body although it is the same Cosmic Energy. It is to this energy that the ancient teachers of Yoga gave the name of Kuṇḍalinī. Writing about Kuṇḍalinī, H. P. Blavatsky says in her *Secret Doctrine* :

> Kundalini Sakti — The power or force which moves in a curved path. It is the Universal Life Principle manifesting energy every where in nature. This force includes the two great forces of attraction and repulsion. Electricity and magnetism are but manifestations of it.

Thus according to her, Kuṇḍalinī is the same Universal or Cosmic Energy just as electricity and magnetism are. Kuṇḍalinī is, however, a greatly loaded word round about which much myth and superstition have gathered. It is elaborately discussed in books of Tantra and of Haṭha Yoga. It is supposed to lie coiled, three and half times, at the base of the spine. It is called Serpent Fire which, when awakened, releases tremendous energy. But its awakening is shrouded in great mystery. The way to its awakening is also a very well-guarded secret which can be obtained only from expert and experienced gurus, and, that too, if they are pleased to reveal it. What is Kuṇḍalinī in Eastern systems of Yoga is similar to Caduceus of the Greek mythology. Normally Prāṇa moves in the body along two channels at the left and the right of the spinal column called Iḍā and Piṅgalā. In the middle is the third channel, Suṣumnā, whose entrance, at the base of the spine, is blocked by Kuṇḍalinī, lying in a coiled position. When it awakens the door of the Suṣumnā, is opened and the Prāṇa energy flows through it. When this happens one is supposed to have reached a sublime state of Yoga.

It the Yoga literature fantastic descriptions are given about the awakening of Kuṇḍalinī and how it rushes to the Crown Cakra at the Head. Kuṇḍalinī is Śakti. She rushes to meet her spouse, Śiva, resting in the area of the Head. When Śiva and Śakti thus meet then is one supposed to be endowed with supernatural powers of great magnitude.

With Kuṇḍalinī is associated the functioning of the Cakras or the Force Centres. These are not in the physical body, but in the Prāṇic or the Etheric Body. There are however certain physical points where the influences of these Cakras are felt. The Cakras are seven in number—Mūlādhāra, Svādhiṣṭhāna, Maṇipūra, Anāhata, Viśuddha, Ājñā and Sahasrāra — the Crown Cakra at the Head. Some authorities speak of a larger number of Cakras and divide them into the Main and the Subsidiary. When Kuṇḍalinī is awakened, the released energy, flowing through the middle channel, Suṣumnā, stimulates each Cakra in turn, finally reaching the Head Cakra. In Tāntrik and Haṭha Yoga books detailed descriptions of the Cakras are given in terms of Lotuses with particular number of petals. Once again round about Cakras also much myth and superstition have grown. One has to sift the wheat from the chaff in order to come to a clear understanding of Kuṇḍalinī and its functioning through the Cakras. In recent years Pandit Gopi Krishna of Kashmir has done much to clarify the issues, ruling out all myth and superstition.

It may be asked : Why have we introduced the subject of Kuṇḍalinī in the midst of our discussion on the transformation of the Human Brain ? We have done it because Kuṇḍalinī is associated with energy, the biological energy, needed by the spiritual aspirant. On the spiritual path man needs energy constantly and also needs to know the process of renewing energy. The subject of energy is introduced in the very first mantra of the Ṛg Veda where the spiritual aspirant invokes Energy in the form of Agni or Fire. The Ṛg Veda says that we put energy in the forefront and therefore worship Agni or Fire. Energy is man's fundamental need as he embarks upon the stupendous journey of spiritual adventure. And Energy is needed at all levels, from the biological to the highest level. But one has to begin at the level of the biological energy before one moves on to subtler levels of spiritual perception. In the awakening of Kuṇḍalinī lies the release of the biological energy, and so we need to turn to it in our studies of meditation.

In the traditional simile of the union of Śiva and Śakti, consequent upon the awakening of Kuṇḍalinī, there is a depth of psychological meaning. Śiva represents the masculine aspect of energy even as Śakti denotes the feminine aspect of the Cosmic Energy. It is in the union of the two that integration comes into being. This integration has to come at all levels. We shall discuss the question of integration at the mental level when we come to that phase of our subject of triple transformation. But just as psychological integration is necessary there has also to be an integration in the biological functioning of the Cosmic Energy too. Energy cannot be released unless the positive and the negative poles meet. In the biological sense, the awakening of Kuṇḍalinī is indicative of the feminine energy merging with the masculine, Śakti meeting Śiva. The Mūlādhāra and the Sahasrāra centres denote respectively the negative and the positive poles in the field of biological energy.

Modern man needs seriously to turn to the question of integration at all levels, for, he is experiencing a state of inner disintegration. This inner integration cannot be brought about by superficial means. It demands a serious approach so that human consciousness, displaying today the masculine aspect, gets permeated by feminine consciousness. It is in the fusion of the masculine and the feminine consciousness that real integration can come into being. In each human individual there must take place a union of Śiva and Śakti. Today at all levels of man's being it is masculine consciousness that is supreme. In this the human brain too is involved, so, that in the functioning of the brain there is perceptible those qualities and characteristics which are fundamentally masculine. It is the masculine brain with all its aggressiveness and argumentativeness that is operating today. There is no wonder in our behaviour-patterns, there are to be seen hardness and cruelty. To ride rough shod on others is considered a mark of success. The human brain is mainly oriented towards competition. All its energies are diverted along that line so that it is on the lookout for evolving such behaviour-patterns and such modes of action as would lead to one's success and other person's defeat. It has to be understood that while the Mind gives direction, it is the Brain which translates these directions into necessary modes of physical action. It may be that the direction given by the mind itself is wrong, but we leave the question of mind and its capacity to give direction to a later chapter. Whether the direction is right or wrong, it is the brain which must translate it into behaviour-patterns. And so if the brain is entirely oriented towards masculine tendencies then it is sure to give that colouring to all its actions and behaviour-patterns. Even the best of mind's directions can be given a wrong turn by such a brain. This is exactly what is happening today in modern civilization. Our noblest organisations seem to be breaking up because of the distortions introduced by Human Brain in implementing their objectives at the level of physical action.

This being the case it is of the highest importance that the brain be energised with such force as carries feminine qualities. The masculine brain is lop-sided gloating over its success along lines of specialization. The brain is much too angular, it must be rounded off so that it acts not only with strength but also with grace. It is this which has rendered the question of Kuṇḍalinī to assume special importance. We have seen that the brain is working at present at a low potential of ten to twelve per cent. If the unused ninety per cent is to be brought into action then the brain must be supplied with great amount of fresh energy.

It is with this energy that new centres of learning can be brought into existence in unused areas of the brain. Without establishing such new reverberating centres, the brain cannot function effectively in an age where changes are taking place at a phenomenally rapid pace. The old brain can ill-serve the needs of the present age. There must be an emergence of a re-vitalised Brain if man is to survive in this new phase of evolutionary growth. Our present brain does not have the capacity of quick adaptation required in this age. And if man cannot adapt himself quickly to fast moving conditions of life, he faces great hazards in the sphere of his survival. Faced with this situation Kuṇḍalinī seems to be the only answer.

As we have stated in the earlier part of this chapter, the subject of Kuṇḍalinī is shrouded in great mystery. By and large, people feel that it is dangerous to turn one's attention to the awakening of Kuṇḍalinī. It should be left to ascetics and to those who renounce the world. It is believed that Kuṇḍalinī is not for the common man. This is due to the fact that the traditional litereture on Kuṇḍalinī does not approach the subject in a scientific manner. The methods for awakening Kuṇḍalinī suggested in Tantra and in Haṭha Yoga are such that ordinary man would be frightened of it. These methods are much too elaborate and cumbrous. They include *āsanas* or physical postures, *prāṇāyāma* or the holding and directing of the breath, *mudrās* or certain physical gestures particularly of the eyes and the tongue, the *Ṣaṭ-Karmas* or sixfold practices which include bodily purification of a very elaborate nature. All these practices require detailed guidance by experts and experienced teachers. It is difficult to find such teachers, and even if one finds them these practices are much too exacting and time-consuming. It would not be safe for one to practise the various items indicated in books of Tantra and Haṭha Yoga by oneself. The physical presence of the teacher is absolutely necessary.

In the Haṭha Yoga and Tāntrik practices the method suggested is a forcible awakening of Kuṇḍalinī. It is through the violent friction between the *Prāṇa* and *Apāna Vāyus* that tremendous heat is generated around the region where Kuṇḍalinī lies coiled.

Due to this friction Kuṇḍalinī is forcibly, and almost violently, awakened. But this is not all. The awakened Kuṇḍalinī has to be directed to each of the Cakras so as to stimulate them and bring them into an active phase. This is done by elaborate practices involving rituals and repetitions of certain *Bīja-mantras*, and concentrating upon each of the Cakras for a considerable length of time. This is an exhausting process and has to be done in the presence of experienced teachers. The friction of *Prāṇa* and *Apāna Vayus*, and the stimulation of Cakras into conditions of activity very often puts the brain out of gear. It does not know how to deal with the new situation. It is an emergency such as it has not known. It is on record that many people who thus forcibly awaken Kuṇḍalinī lose their balance and are unable to behave in a normal manner. Their bodily needs increase a great deal — the needs of hunger or of sex or both. They tend to become indolent because of brain's incapacity to deal with a situation to which it has been suddenly called. There are great hazards for the brain and the body in the forcible and violent practices for the awakening of Kuṇḍalinī. It is because of this that most people are frightened at the very name of Kuṇḍalinī and its awakening.

There is another important factor to be noted in the practices of forcible and violent way of awakening Kuṇḍalinī, and that is its underlying purpose. The main purpose in Kuṇḍalinī awakening in Haṭha Yoga and Tāntrik practices is to develop super-physical powers, or powers of lower psychism. People are greatly attracted by the prospects of the development of such powers. There are teachers in modern times, as there have been in the past too, who practise *Śakti-pāta* whereby a teacher is supposed to awaken Kuṇḍalinī in his disciples by touch or by sight or by mantra or even by thought. Now the awakening of Kuṇḍalinī, by such method if that is possible, is fraught with still more dangers. Without gradually widening the brain potential and without proper spiritual foundation, the awakening of Kuṇḍalinī is most dangerous. To dabble in the attempt at forcible development psychic powers is itself most hazardous. There must be some other way of awakening Kuṇḍalinī, the way that is safer, and such as does not make an aspirant dependent on a teacher or a guru. After discussing the traditional ways of awakening Kuṇḍalinī, Sri Aurobindo says in *Letters on Yoga* :

> ...this is the method of Tantra. In our Yoga (Integral Yoga) it is not necessary to go through the systemetised method. It takes place spontaneously.

Here Sri Aurobindo speaks of the spontaneous way of awakening Kuṇḍalinī as against the forcible way of Tantra and Haṭha Yoga. However, we do not find any elaboration in the writings of Sri Aurobindo as to what this spontaneous way is. We are certainly greatly helped by his mentioning a way other than the forcible way of Haṭha Yoga and Tantra. One mus probe into the matter as to what can be the spontaneous way of awakening Kùṇḍalinī. It should be borne in mind that the spontaneous way is not necessarily the easy way—it may be a more difficult way. But the spontaneous way is one where the individual, by his own effort and without depending upon any external agency, can awaken Kuṇḍalinī. Besides, it is bound to be free from hazards and dangers as lie along the path of forcible methods of awakening the Serpent Fire. Sri Aurobindo says that it is not necessary to go through a systematised method. This means it cannot be by the friction of *Prāṇa* and *Apāna* and by concentrating on one Cakra after the other. From the above passage of Sri Aurobindo it appears that there is a more flexible way of awakening Kuṇḍalinī. Surely it would be worthwhile to find out what this flexible approach to the awakening of Kuṇḍalinī is.

In this age of science and technology we are familiar with the release of atomic energy. A tiny atom contains tremendous energy which when released can give to man an atomic bomb or can enable him to employ it for peaceful purposes. In this task of releasing atomic energy, the one method adopted is that of Fission. This implies the breaking up of atoms in which the nucleus of an atom has to be split into two by bombarding it with neutrons. It is this method of fission with nuclear chain reactions that was used for the manufacture of atom bomb which brought the second world war to an end after enacting one of the greatest tragedies of human history. But there is another method also for obtaining energy from the atomic nucleus. It is a method of Fusion, instead of Fission. Here the nuclei of two light elements are induced to come together in a condition of fusion. The inducement is done by intensive heat. When these two light nuclei come together then there is a release of energy. In the sun, energy is produced not by Fission but by Fusion of the hydrogen nuclie to form helium. It is said that intensive heat is necessary in order to bring light particles close enough to each other. To cause them to fuse they have to be accelerated to enormous speeds. Alan Issacs in his book *Introducing Science* says :

> The only Fusion reactions that have so far been brought about by man are those of the Hydrogen bomb .... It should be noted that while fission bombs are limited in size....hydrogen bombs can be made of virtually any size...It will be remembered that the Hiroshima bomb was said to be equivalent to 20 Kilotons (20,000 tons) of TNT, current models of the hydrogen bombs are rated at about 20 megatons (20 million tons) of TNT.

Thus the Fusion bombs seem to be more powerful than the Fission bombs in energy content. By inducing two light elements to come together there comes into being thermonuclear reactions where the release of energy is greatly enhanced. At present all over the world experiments are being made to harness this thermonuclear energy for peaceful purposes. Alan Issacs says :

> Fusion reactions have the great advantage over Fission reactions in that they use as fuel the plentiful element hydrogen, instead of relatively scarce element Uranium. The sea is full of water, every molecule of which contains two atoms of hydrogen !

Thus release of ene gy by the method of Fusion seems to be a simpler device inspite of the difficulty of intense heat required to bring the two light elements together. A simple device need not necessarily be easy — but if difficulties are surmounted then the energy release is enormous, and that too from an element which is to be found in plenty.

It may be asked why have we introduced the subject of nuclear energy by Fission and Fusion in the midst of a discussion on the awakening of Kuṇḍalinī. We have done this because the awakening of Kuṇḍalinī also implies release of energy, of biological energy, which is only another form of that Cosmic Energy of which nuclear energy is also one of the manifestations. We have seen that the trad tional way of releasing the energy stored in Kuṇḍalinī is forcible and violent. We have also noted that there are dangers and hazards involved in this forcible awakening of Kuṇḍalinī. We turned our enquiry to the question as to whether there can be another way of awakening Kuṇḍalinī, a way that is simple and spontaneous. The forcible and violent method of arousing Kuṇḍalini is akin to the Fission method of releasing nuclear energy. The friction that is generated by the *Prāṇa* and *Apāna Vayus* is akin to the bombardment of an atom by neutrons as seen in the manufacture of the atom bomb. Just as there is the method of Fusion applied in the release of the thermonuclear energy there may also be the Fusion-way of awakening Kuṇḍalinī. If so, the energy released will be very great, and it will come about by the fusing of elements, and not by the process of splitting as is the case in the chain reaction of the atom bomb. We are told that in the Fusion method two elements are induced to come together by the application of a great intensity of heat. It would be fruitful to probe this question whether there could be a fusion-way of awakening Kuṇḍalinī as against the Fission-way which is employed in the traditional practices, the nature of which we have already discussed. It is obvious that the Fusion way would be gentle, and not violent as one finds in the forcible awakening of Kuṇḍalinī.

The Kuṇḍalinī energy can be released so as to take the aspirant along the path of Lower Psychism where certain super-physical powers of Siddhis can be developed. But it can also be released for entering a new dimension of living, a healthy, creative, spiritual life away from tensions and conflicts. Either one moves along the path of spiritualism or one moves along the path of spirituality. Since the fundamental need of modern man is to explore the way of healthy, creative living he must move along the spiritual and not the spiritualistic path. The way of spiritualism opens out by the forcible, the fission way, of awakening Kuṇḍalinī. The way of spirituality reveals itself along the spontaneous, the Fusion-way of releasing the Kuṇḍalinī energy. But what is this spontaneous way and how is one to tread it ?

SEVEN

THE FESTIVE OCCASION

THERE is a commonly held belief that one who wishes to tread the spiritual path must regard himself as a candidate for Woe. He must be ready to receive larger and larger share of suffering and sorrow as he passes through trials and tribulations which must be his lot from the moment he decides to tread the spiritual path. If suffering does not come in his life then he feels that there is something wrong in his spiritual endeavour. Both in the East and the West suffering has been regarded as a badge that gives entry into spiritual life. Perhaps this element of sorrow and suffering entered the field of spiritual life after Buddhist doctrines influenced the thinking of philosophers. One finds this element of suffering and sorrow emphasised in Christian approaches too. It is only as the spiritual aspirant is burnt in the fire of suffering that he emerges purified. It is this idea of suffering that introduced into certain religious practices elements of masochism and sadism. Either the religious man inflicts suffering on himself, or he takes delight in inflicting suffering on others.

It is only when we turn to the saints and mystics that we find an entirely different atmosphere of spiritual life. They have all the time talked of joy and delight. They move about with the intoxication of sublime bliss. They have not indicated that the spiritual path is a bed of roses, nor have they suggested that it is an easy path. Though not easy, they have indicated a simple way, bereft of all the complexities of the mind. They have shown the way to the Everest of life, and surely the mountain path that leads to it is not easy. But such is the ecstasy and intoxication of the mystic that for him the idea that the path is rugged and steep does not even once arise. Addressing the spiritual aspirant, H. P. Blavatsky says in her *Voice of the Silence*:

> Thou canst not travel on the Path
> before thou hast become that path itself.

The mystics who sing the songs of the dawn even in the midst of the night are able to do so because they have become the path itself. The traveller will find the path irksome if he feels himself as different from the path. The traveller becoming the path is a non-dual experience. In such experience there is neither the Way-farer nor the Way, there is only the walking, the pure movement. When this experience comes, how can there be anything but joy? When there is pure walking, no question of reaching the destination arises. It is the reaching of the destination that makes the movement on the Path tiring and irksome. The mystics of all ages have moved on the spiritual path, bursting out in songs, because for them there was no question of arriving at some destination. C. Jinarajadasa, a former president of The Theosophical Society, says in one of his poems:

> What is the spiritual life, my friend?
> It is to see the end in the beginning.

The mystics have seen the end even before they started the journey and so the end was all the time there as they moved on the Path. The end was not away; it was all the time giving company to the Way-farer as he moved on. God is not away from man; He walks with man as he journeys along the spiritual path. In such an experience how can there be any place for sorrow and suffering ? If the Beloved is there with the Lover all the time on the journey, then where is the question of reaching the destination?

It is unfortunate that Woe and Suffering have been brought into the question of man's treading the spiritual path. It has been a later development in the history of spiritual life in India. If we turn to the Vedas and the Upaniṣads it is joy that is the undercurrent of spiritual life. The Upaniṣads speak of *Ānandam Brahma*, Brahman is joy itself. The Īśāvāsya Upaniṣad tells us that the whole universe is pervaded by *Īśa* or God. It says that even in the fleeting things of life, He resides. One of the great truths propounded by the Upaniṣads is: *Sarvam-khalu-idam-Brahma*, meaning All is Brahman If so, where is the place for suffering and sorrow? Among the Modern Indian thinkers, Sri Aurobindo has laid emphasis on *Ānanda* as the very foundation of the Universe. He says that if God created the Universe out of love, then how can there be anything but joy in that Universe. He says again and again that the Creator can be found only in His creation and nowhere else. If the creator is in His creation, then surely the manifested universe must be a place of joy and delight. In the Bhagavad Gītā also, while talking of the spiritual man, Śrī Kṛṣṇa says that 'he who sees Me everywhere and everything in me, is a true devotee who never leaves me nor do I leave him'. If these have been the ideas of spiritual life given to us by ancient seers and sages, then how did suffering and sorrow got associated with spiritual life?

It is in the later philosophical thought of India that the idea of the world being a snare and Māyā came into vogue. Under this ideology, renunciation became the hall-mark of spiritual life. More and more people were told to shun the world because it was a snare. Those who renounced the world and became ascetics began to be respected more and more. For seeking Reality one must get away from the world and its activities— this was propounded by learned men. Severe mortification of the flesh and rigorous austerities became the rule of spiritual life. If *Īśa* or the Lord pervades the entire universe, what is one to renounce? He resides, and that too in His fullness, even in the things that are sought to be renounced. It is obvious that the gospel of suffering and woe which found currency in the later philosophical thought was a negation of the teachings of the Upaniṣads which form the very bedrock of Indian culture.

We have been considering the question of the awakening of Kuṇḍalinī. The traditional practices are violent, aiming at a forcible awakening of the Serpent Fire. And yet it is said that in the awakening of Kuṇḍalinī, there takes place the union of Śiva and Śakti. Has this union to be forcible and violent ? Has Śakti to be awakened by such means ? The union of Śiva and Śakti is a festive occasion where anything forcible or violent has no place whatsoever. Śakti has to be gently awakened so that she can meet her spouse in an atmosphere of joy and festivity, and not in conditions of austerity and violence. But one finds this festive spirit completely absent in the traditional Haṭha Yoga practices for the awakening of Kuṇḍalinī. It is true that in Tāntrik practices the element of joy was present but then its practices soon became degenerated. We shall see in the next chapter why these practices got so degenerated. And so the only method now prescribed for the awakening of Kuṇḍalinī, which has respectability, is the Haṭha Yoga practices which we have described in the last chapter. But these practices breathe the air not of festivity but of forcible awakening. We have asked ourselves a question : Is there any other way where Kuṇḍalinī is awakened spontaneously under conditions that are appropriate for the festive occasion of the Union of Śiva and Śakti ?

In the awakening of Kuṇḍalinī what takes place is the release of biological energy. This happens because of the negative and the positive poles of our biological mechanism being induced to come together. It is a known fact that the like poles repel, but the unlike poles attract. The *Mūlādhāra* Cakra is where Kuṇḍalinī lies coiled. If it is stimulated then the positive pole which is *Sahasrāra* will experience a union with the negative pole. It is when this happens that energy is available to the body, to the entire biological entity. This release is experienced in the brain, and so, the brain is endowed with a great deal of released energy with which it brings the unused portions into operation.

It is our common experience that when we are happy we feel more energetic. Somehow from somewhere this energy seems to be giving to the whole body a sense of expansion. We feel as if we could distribute our largess generously to an ever increasing number of people. We like to extend our sphere of activity. There is a feeling of adventure. Our whole behaviour towards persons changes so that we like to include more and more people in our sphere of influence. This mysterious release of energy takes place all the time when we are in moments of happiness. There is a feeling of 'moreness' in our biological make-up. As against this when we pass through unpleasant events and experience pain, our attitude is characterised by withdrawal. We would like to return to our own shell, shunning all company. Thus pain brings a feeling of contraction while happiness gives us a sense of expansion. During pain we have less energy at our disposal, but during pleasure the energy seems to be plentiful. While in moments of pleasure we are out-going, in moments of pain we seem to shrink within ourselves. One can safely surmise that happiness contains a secret of releasing more energy.

The energy released during moments of happiness is obviously the biological energy, for, the body feels energetic only through that energy. Now the storehouse of biological energy is Kuṇḍalinī. And it is quite possible that in moments of happiness, unconsciously, some of the Kuṇḍalinī energy is released — may be just a trickle. It is a mistaken idea that Kuṇḍalinī can be released only in a massive flow. The trickles of this energy do get released due to which sometimes the brain feels greatly stimulated. Most of us have experienced sudden activity in the brain due to which we are able to do things which we have not done. Very often the energy released during moments of happiness is frittered away or dissipated so that the brain receives no advantage from such release. But the very fact that in moments of happiness extra energy is experienced shows that some stimulation of Kuṇḍalinī does take place. If this phenomenon could be explored further, perhaps we may be able to come to a spontaneous way of awakening Kuṇḍalinī so that the energy-release is not just in trickles but in great bulk. It can also be explored as to how the dissipation of this energy could be prevented so that the brain gets its full force for its task of bringing the unused area into operation. If this could be explored then we will know how to bring the brain to work at its full potential.

The release of energy during moments of happiness can be compared to the release of nuclear energy through Fusion. In happiness we get fused with our environment. There is no fission caused by friction. Our problem is twofold. Can we release energy in this Fusion-way, and can this released energy be prevented from being frittered away or dissipated ? The release of energy along the way of happiness would be free from violence and force. It will be a pleasant and a gentle way of awakening Kuṇḍalinī. In its act of awakening there will be spontaneity. This gentle way may or may not be attended by the development of psychic powers but it will certainly lead to a new way of living. There will be creativity and fullness because of the full potential of the brain operating upon the situations of life.

We have referred in these pages to the writings of Pandit Gopi Krishna of Kashmir. There is a book by him entitled *Kuṇḍalinī: The Evolutionary Energy in Man.* It contains a detailed description of his own experiences in Kuṇḍalinī-awakening. While it makes interesting reading, it does not make a happy reading. The whole description has elements of morbidity in it. Besides, he does not reveal any method of awakening the Serpent Fire. He no doubt rules out the traditional way of forcible awakening contained in Haṭha Yoga practices. But he does not tell us what is the alternative way, not forcible, but spontaneous.

It may be asked, what would be the distinguishing marks in the behaviour of one in whom Kuṇḍalinī has awakened ? We know that along the forcible way, through Haṭha Yoga, when Kuṇḍalinī is aroused, there are to be seen certain superphysical powers. If along the spontaneous or the Fusion way, the development of psychic powers is not involved, then what is it that distinguishes the man in whom Kuṇḍalinī has been aroused ? Such a man has quick adaptability to outer challenges due to the activisation of wider areas of the brain. There is a maturity in such an individual, for, he is no longer the creature of the herd. There is an effulgence in his body, vitalised as it is by the flow of new energy. He has wider and wider contacts with life, and is able to move about in a variety of fields, subtle and intangible, so far as life's expressions are concerned. His powers of communication are greatly intensified so that he is able to communicate with others with clarity and simplicity. Such an individual has tremendous powers of absorption so that his brain is ready to receive sense impacts as they arrive from all the sense organs. Due to this increased receptivity of the brain, the senses too grow in their greater sensitivity. Thus such a man is able to live a fuller life in a universe that is much wider than what we know. He is one in whom the process of Individuation has started, to use the phrase from the writings of Carl G. Jung. He is as it were on tbe point of stepping out of mere mediocrity so that he is no longer one among others in the crowd. P. W. Martin in his book *Experiment in Depth* says :

> ....Individuation needs to be distinguished from Individualism. It is true that in the individuation process, a man becomes a being in his own right, differentiated from the mass. But individuation is also the means by which a new and deeper relationship is made with others. Without this new and deeper relationship there is no wholeness.

Thus in a man in whom Kuṇḍalinī has been awakened by the spontaneous way there are to be seen these two traits. He steps out of the herd and becomes an individual, but he also becomes integrated in a deeper way with all that lives, with the entire environment. The author of the above book further on says :

> Considered analytically, individuation consists of a two-way movement : on the one hand, a process of separating, of differentiation; on the other a process of coming together, of integration. In order to 'get from where you are not' it is necessary to separate those things which prevent you from being yourself. In order to 'arrive where you are' it is necessary to

bring together those things which enable you to become yourself.

In other words the man in whom Kuṇḍalinī has been awakened, in the spontaneous manner, comes into his own. He is enabled to lead his own life, receiving in ample measure the sense impacts from the sense organs, and receiving also in full measure the instructions and directions from the mind. He has the capacity to contain them all, and organise actions and behaviour-patterns in a manner he had not known before.

But the question still remains : Are there practical steps by treading which one can come to the safe and spontaneous awakening of Kuṇḍalinī ? If so, what are those steps ? It is to this question that we must turn in the next chapter.

EIGHT

THE NEGATIVE AND THE POSITIVE

IN AN earlier chapter we described the Human Brain as a Bridge between the Mind and the Body. At present this bridge is much too rickety to carry all the traffic that must pass over it. The strengthening of the bridge has become an imperative need today. In a world where outer changes are taking place at the rapid pace, the brain has to be very alert and competent to receive all the sense impacts, process them and pass them on as percepts to the Mind. It has also to receive instructions from the Mind and issue necessary orders for their execution. This twofold work has increased considerably today because of the nature of the technological society in which we live. The brain must be very quick to adapt itself to fast moving conditions of life. Unfortunately the brain, as it is functioning today, is unable to discharge these duties effectively and efficiently. This is so because only ten per cent of the Brain potential is in use; ninety per cent is unused. This ninety per cent must be harnessed. But, for this, the brain potential has to be increased. It is here that we are faced with the problem of increased energy that must be at the disposal of the brain if the un-used ninety per cent of its potential has to be put into operation. Since by the awakening of Kuṇḍalinī alone this energy is available, we have to examine, rationally and scientifically, the question of the arousal of the Serpent Fire. Our concern, one and the only, in approaching the question of Kuṇḍalinī-awakening is for exploring the possibility of increasing the brain-potential. We are not interested in the development of psychic powers which have been ordinarily associated with the arousal of Kuṇḍlinī.

In order to fulfil our main, and the only aim, we have to rule out the traditional Haṭha Yoga way of awakening Kuṇḍalinī. We have called it the Fission Way. We are exploring the Fusion way or the spontaneous way of awakening Kuṇḍalinī. We saw in the last chapter that somehow in moments of happiness we have increased biological energy at our disposal. We feel more energetic when we have the experience of happiness. It is quite possible that during moments of happiness there is some trickle of energy release from Kuṇḍalinī. But this cannot serve our purpose. We have to find out whether it is possible to use the way of happiness more consciously for the release of greater energy, and whether it is possible to see that this released energy does not get frittered away or dissipated in any manner whatsoever.

Before we proceed further with this inquiry, we must be clear about the functions of the Mind and the Brain. We live on the physical plane and so our actions have to be on that plane. Our relationships with others have to express themselves in behaviour-patterns at the physical level. Now every such physical action has two components. One is the content of action, and the other is the structure of action. There is no doubt that the content of action is supplied by the Mind. We are not going into the question as to what is the nature of this content. We will leave it for discussion in subsequent chapters. We are concerned here with the function of the Brain. Obviously one of its main functions is to give shape and form to the content given by the mind. The brain must give appropriate structure in terms of physical actions to the content supplied by the Mind. Now if the Brain is ill-equipped then its structures will be shabby, without clear outlines. It will be slip-shod, showing forth elements of disorder. But if the brain is fully equipped then its structures and forms will be tidy and orderly. Since our brain at present functions at a low potential, our actions do not show forth always that neatness, and tidiness, that order and symmetry which they should show. It is of the highest importance that the structures of our action and behaviour-patterns should be neat and tidy. But this can happen only when the brain-potential is increased. We discussed in the last chapter the question of the Individuation process. In terms of the brain, this means, that in the functioning of the brain there must be a distinct quality, an individuality. Sometimes we see a person performing a small action, but giving to that action a distinctness. One sees in such an action a stamp of an efficient and an orderly brain. But very often persons performing big actions do so in such a disorderly manner that one recoils from it. It is the mind which gives matter or content, but it is the brain that evolves the manner of translating that matter or content into physical actions and behaviour.

Our concern in considering the question of Kuṇḍalinī-awakening is to see that the bridge between the Mind and the Body gets enormously strengthened so that it can discharge its function of supplying neat and orderly structures most efficiently. In other words, our interest in the subject of Kuṇḍalinī centres round increasing the brain-potential so that the ninety per cent of the unused areas of the brain may be brought into full operation. And in this task, while ruling out traditional methods of awakening Kuṇḍalinī, we are enquiring as to whether experience of happy moments could be employed consciously and systematically both for the release of energy and for preventing its dissipation. The process of individuation must start first with the brain and then move further in the direction of transforming the Mind too. How is the brain to be transformed so that its potential increases enabling it to deal with situations arising in the modern world, with great efficiency ?

With regard to increasing the Brain-potential there are two factors to be borne in Mind. First, Variety and second, Intensity. The scientists have mapped out the areas of the brain and have located centres for different sense-impacts. There are centres of hearing, of sight, of taste, of touch and of smell. John Pfeiffer in his book *The Human Brain* says :

> These tiny organs — the ears, eyes, nose, tongue — are some of your windows in the outside world. Reports about the state of

things inside your body come from other built-in sense organs which give rise to sensations of muscular tension, hunger, thirst, nausea. The number of senses is not known exactly. It is certainly more than five, and probably somewhere around twenty.

Each sensation goes to the appointed centre in the Brain. There is no confusion about it. The music that we hear goes to the hearing centre, and not to the sight centre. If this were to happen then we would see music, not hear it ! But this never happens. However, the brain's receptivity with regard to sense reports is limited due to the low potential at which it is working. This low potential of the brain has also affected the working of the senses. One must re-educate the senses as one must see to the increase of the brain potential. The re-education of the senses is a comparatively easy undertaking, and so it can be tackled first. With the increase in the brain potential further education of the senses will take place. But even within the existing brain-potential the education of the senses can and must take place, What do we mean by this preliminary education of the senses ?

Our range of sense-receptivity is at present very limited. The subtle nuances, the delicate differences, of life's impacts at present pass unnoticed. We hear only certain sounds. Sounds below or beyoud that range are not picked up by us. Similarly we see only certain range of colours. All of us, in a sense, are colour-blind, because certain shades of colours are unperceived by us. The same applies to touch and taste and smell. Now one can consciously extend the range of sense-receptivity. This is what is meant by the preliminary education of the senses. We say preliminary because with the increase in brain-potential, a wider education of the senses will come into existence, naturally and spontaneously.

What is the conscious effort that one can employ to increase the receptivity-range of the senses ? One can first find out one's range with reference to the five senses. We hear certain pitches of sound, low as well as high. The same about the eyes. One can experiment by first listening to lower and still lower pitches.

One can also experiment with sounds that are near and sounds that are far. How much low in one's hearing of the sound-pitch can one go, and how much of the distant sounds can one pick up ? And can one increase this distance ? One can experiment with the sense of sight trying to find out how many shades of colour can one see, and can one extend the range ? One can make similar experiments with touch and taste and smell. Take for example the Nose, the most neglected of our sense organs. In an article entitled '*Your Educated Nose*' adapted from the book *The Sense of Smell*, the author Roy Bedicheck says:

> Most school systems have art teachers educating the eye and the music teachers educating the ear, but none so far has attempted to tutor the nose. Yet the nose holds the key to distinctions no other sense can unlock, and to aesthetic pleasures as great for some, as music and pictures are for others.

It would be a fascinating experiment to become one's own tutor so far as the education of the various senses is concerned. When nothing special is to be done, one can quietly sit or lie down gradually extending the range of sense-receptivity. And this can be done without bothering about the increase in brain potential. This process of sense education will be a prelude to the bigger task of increasing the brain-potential, and it will be an appropriate prelude. One will begin to live in a larger world before that larger world is enlarged still more by the increase in the brain-potential. Thus the re-education of the senses will be the first step in the direction of breaking down the barriers that compel us to live in a restricted world. The second step will be the increasing of the brain potential so that the whole of the brain functions, and, not just a part of it, as is the case at present.

In this work of intensifying the brain potential, we have to see to it that the twin-principle of Intensity and Variety is not lost sight of. So far as Intensity is concerned it is through the way of happiness that one must move. But happiness is a vague word which does not clearly denote the biological state concerned.

Perhaps the word pleasure would be more appropriate as a biological experience of happiness. Since we are discussing the question of the release of Kuṇḍalinī, the biological energy, it would be well for us to go into the functioning of the pleasure-principle. Pleasure is something with which we are all familiar, for, it comes within the sensorial experience. It is by undestanding the pleasure-principle that we will be enabled to comprehend the fusion-way of releasing energy. The experience of pleasure gives to our biological mechanism a feeling of energy and vitality. In moments of pleasure we feel bodily more energetic, and less tired. Unfortunately in the so-called spiritual disciplines pleasure has been totally banned; in fact, pleasure is considered as something positively anti-spiritual. To feel pleasure is something natural to a human being. If spiritual discipline does not start from something that is natural then it will be a forced discipline leading to tiredness and frustration. In order to go far in spiritual endeavour it is best to start from the base of something that is natural. And surely Pleasure and Pain are the most natural experiences of a human individual. But since Pain sucks up one's energy, and Pleasure releases energy, for the purposes of Kuṇḍalinī awakening, it is the avenue of pleasure that needs to be explored.

But one may ask : Has not Tantra advocated the way of pleasure in its spiritual sādhana or discipline ? In Tantra *Yoga* and *Bhoga* have to be co-existent if one wishes to move into spiritual realms. The word *Bhoga* means enjoyment. And so Tāntrik practices have recognised the basis of pleasure-principle in undertaking spiritual discipline. But we know that Tāntrik disciplines degenerated into immoral practices and sex-orgies. It is because of this degeneration that Tantra became a word to be shunned in any serious spiritual practice.

Why did the Tāntrik practices degenerate into sex-orgies, and how do we know that following the pleasure-principle in awakening Kuṇḍalinī will not lead us the same way once again ? Pleasure is born of desire, and there is nothing wrong in having desires. To have desires is natural for a living being. One might as well say that the mind of a living person should not have thoughts. Thoughts are bound to arise in the mind of a person who is alive. Similarly desires are bound to arise in the life of a living individual. To have no desires is to be a skeleton, psychologically squeezed out, having no vitality nor any energy. Surely one cannot go to the door of Reality as a skeleton. In such a state one will not have any energy to experience even the impact of Reality. It is not desire that is wrong; it is the transformation of desire into craving which presents us with problems on the spiritual path. To have desire and yet not transform it into craving — it is this which needs to be understood if one is to tread the spiritual path joyously and not with tiredness and boredom. Yoga does not mean the killing of all thoughts and desires; it means coming to a state where thoughts and desires arise but they are given no continuity. When desire is given a continuity then it becomes a craving. In *Light on the Path*, a profound book of Theosophical Mysticism, the following instructions are given to the spiritual aspirant :

> Desire that which is within you
> Desire that which is beyond you
> Desire that which is unattainable.

But these three instructions are followed by another directive which says :

> Kill out desire of life.

Asking the aspirant to have desires and yet also instructing him to kill out desire is most confusing. These instructions can be understood only when one makes a distinction between Desire and Craving — to have desire and yet not to allow it to become a craving, this is what is demanded of the aspirant.

It is in the feeling of pleasure that one experiences a release of biological energy. If there could be pleasure and yet give no continuity to it — then the released energy could not only be intensified but it can be used for whatever purpose one has in view. It is when a continuity is given to pleasure that degeneration starts. It is not the feeling of the pleasure that creates a problem in spiritual life, it is the giving of continuity to it which raises immense difficulties on the spiritual path. In the Tāntrik practices when this warning was not heeded pleasure resulted in demoralization and sex orgies.

What do we mean by not giving a continuity to pleasure? Pleasure obviously implies enjoyment. If there could be Enjoyment without Indulgence then surely we will have the increased energy released in moments of pleasure and yet there will not happen a degeneration caused by pursuing the pleasure-principle as has been witnessed in Tāntrik practices. There is a mistaken idea that experience of pleasure at the bodily level can be only sex-pleasure. Although sex-pleasure is not excluded, it does not exhaust the sphere of pleasure at the biological level. In fact, Enjoyment without Indulgence must mean moving from the Sensual to the Sensuous in the field of pleasure. When this movement takes place then pleasure transforms itself into joy, thence Delight. From Delight this movement, of Enjoyment without Indulgence, comes to Rapture and then to the experience of Bliss and Ecstasy. This movement begins with pleasure, for, that is the only beginning which a man can make. If pleasure is not given a continuity then this movement to Joy, Delight, Rapture, Bliss and Ecstasy takes place spontaneously. As we have stated earlier, it is not pleasure that is evil, it is the giving of continuity to pleasure that is evil. If one feels intense pleasure about, or, in, anything, but refrains from indulgence, then the intensity of pleasure grows as the movement of pleasure culminates in bliss and ecstasy. During all the intervening steps the intensity grows tremendously. That which prevents intensity from coming into being is indulgence. In Indulgence the energy released by pleasure is dissipated or frittered away, and so there can be no further movement to joy, and delight, to rapture and bliss, and thence to ecstasy.

When there is enjoyment without indulgence then the intensity of pleasure increases, and it is this intensity which initiates the movement from the sensual to the sensuous, from pleasure to bliss and ecstasy. When there is enjoyment with indulgence then the feeling of pleasure degenerates into excitement, and excitement is always exhausting. In this exhaustion energy gets dissipated, and so at the end of pleasure one is almost laid low. There is a gulf of difference between Intensity and Excitement. Strangely though it may seem, intensity generates more energy, it is like the generation of energy by Fusion. In the earlier chapter we saw that for Fusion two light elements are induced to come together. But this is possible only when there is intensity of heat. We are considering the awakening of Kuṇḍalinī by the Fusion Way. And so intensity is a *sine qua non* in releasing Kuṇḍalinī energy. This intensity is supplied by Enjoyment without indulgence. In this, enjoyment is not slowed down; in fact, it is at its peak, but it is not allowed to fritter itself away in acts of indulgence. Now Indulgence and Resistance are two sides of the same medallion, for, when we resist it is for indulgence in its opposite. If there is Enjoyment without resistance or indulgence then pleasure reaches its height of intensity. In this pure intensity, sensual is burnt away and the sensuous comes into being. In other words the movement from pleasure to joy, delight, rapture, bliss and ecstasy begins.

One may ask : What is indulgence, and how does it project itself in one's experience of pleasure ? Indulgence is an act of holding on to the event or the experience or the object, we are unable to let it go. We cannot end the experience at any moment, certainly not at the peak of the experience. Indulgence is an act of giving an extension in time to objects and events of pleasure. We leave off pleasure only when we feel satiated for the time being, or when we are exhausted, or when we feel bored and tired. To leave off pleasure in such a state is to put it away when one is enervated or when one's energy has already been dissipated. It is only when we have no more energy left that, for the time being, we move away from objects of pleasure or we end temporarily the event that had given us pleasure. In such indulgence it is obvious that there is no energy left for the movement, from the sensual to the sensuous. When an event or an experience or an object of pleasure is put away at the height of experiencing then what remains is pure intensity unrelated to events and objects. In the ending of experience at such a point one is enabled to move with intensity that is not circumscribed by events and objects. Intensity is extracted from pleasurable experiences when such experiences are at their height or at their peak. To be able to step out of an experience when it is at its peak is to be endowed with tremendous intensity comparable to the intensity needed in the fusion-way of generating energy. It is only in such intensity that Śiva and Śakti can be induced to come together; it is in such intensity that the two poles, the negative and the positive, come together to generate energy. In some occult books it is said that Kuṇḍalinī lies covering the Heart. This seems strange because ordinarily Kuṇḍalinī is supposed to lie near the base of the spine. Between the base of the spine and the heart there is no nearness. But heart in this context is not to be understood in physical terms. Heart signifies feeling. To say that Kuṇḍalinī lies covering the Heart is to imply that it is waiting for the intensity of heart to awaken it. When intensity is divested of all its associations with events or objects then there is the end of indulgence. This is possible when one can end an experience, even the most pleasant, in a split second without any lingering look at the event or the object left behind. If one is listening to music, or standing in front of nature's beauty, or if one is reading an absorbing book...can one leave this in the midst of greatest enjoyment and that too without a wrench or a pull ? This includes all experiences which give biological pleasure to the person. To be able to end an experience at the point of its highest pleasurability is to be free from indulgence. In his London Talks of 1965, J. Krishnamurti poses the following question :

> How does one come to a point where in the full enjoyment of something, one ends it ?

To be able to end one's association or identification with something in the very moment of its full enjoyment is to know Enjoyment without Indulgence. It is in such enjoyment that the end comes in the moment of full intensity. Then it is the Intensity that remains, for what is ended is one's association or indentification with an object or an event. To extract pure Intensity out of enjoyment is to initiate the movement from the sensual to the sensuous.

The sensual experience is not necessarily the sex experience. Any experience can become sensual. Similarly any experience can become sensuous. The sensuous experience belongs purely to the senses. It is in the sensual experience that mind or thought enters. The senses by themselves do not get attached to any experience or event. It is the entry of thought that asks the senses to linger at one point or not to linger at any particular point. It is from this that senses are instructed to get attached. And so it is the entry of thought that makes a sensuous experience sensual. The factor of indulgence in the midst of enjoyment is the product of thought. It is thought which gives continuity to pleasure. It is mind that does not allow any experience to end at the point of highest intensity. It asks for more and more of a particular experience just as it asks for less and less with reference to some other experience. In the Second Discourse of the Bhagavad Gītā there is a significant verse which says :

> He attaineth Peace into whom all desires flow as rivers flow into the ocean, which is filled with water, but remaineth unmoved — not he who desireth desires.

In terms of this verse it is not desire that creates a problem. In fact the verse says that he into whom all desires flow even as rivers flow into the ocean knows what Peace of mind is. The problem arises when one desireth desires. It is with the entry of thought in the field of desire that the desiring of desires begins. It is this which renders that which is sensuous into that which is sensual. Even the listening to music, or engaging in painting, or reading a book, or anything else can become sensual with the entry of thought in its enjoyment. Enjoyment without indulgence is verily Enjoyment without the Enjoyer. It is hardly necessary to point out that it is Mind which is the Enjoyer. The intensity brought about by pleasure gets tremendously more intensified when there is Enjoyment without the Enjoyer, when the factor of indulgence does not enter the experiencing of pleasure. As the intensity initiated by pleasure grows, it reaches its heights in bliss and ecstasy. Under the impact of this intensity

Kuṇḍalinī awakens in a gentle manner. Its energy, negative in character, moves on to the *Sahasrāra*, where the union of Śakti with Śiva takes place. It is after this union that new energy is available to the brain and through it to the entire body. Unless the negative and the positive meet there can be no energy available for the rejuvenation of the brain as well as the entire biological mechanism. In the spontaneous way, the intensity, generated by pleasure and heightened on its sensuous way, induces the union of Śakti and Śiva. This is indeed the fusion way. In its upward flow Kuṇḍalinī touches the various Cakras or Force centres but does not halt there. In this slight touch by Kuṇḍalinī the cakras are no doubt stimulated, but they do not get activised for proper functioning. It is only when Kuṇḍalinī descends from Sahasrāra, after her union with Śiva, that it activises one by one the various cakras thus releasing their functional activities. In the traditional way of Haṭha Yoga, Kuṇḍalinī stops at each cakra on its upward journey. This practice may be for the development of psychic powers, but surely it does not result in the activisation of the unused portions of the brain, nor does it give new energy and vitality to the biological mechanism. In this method the purpose is to vitalize the various cakras with the help of Kuṇḍalinī. But in the spontaneous way about which we have been discussing, the fundamental purpose is the re-vitalization of the brain and the body. And so Kuṇḍalinī in its ascent moves on to the positive pole of Sahasrāra. It is in its descent that the various cakras get slowly activised. This is Kuṇḍalinī operating from Above, and not from Below.

It may be asked, and, rightly, that if Kuṇḍalinī is awakened through the intensity, initiated by the experience of pleasure, but, without allowing the factor of indulgence to enter, is not the spiritual aspirant made to depend upon the moments of pleasure over which he has no control ? After all moments of pleasure cannot be ordered about, they come when they choose to come. Thus a person has to depend upon the whims and fancies of outer circumstance. The moments of pleasure may come suddenly or they may not come for a long time. And so the method of awakening Kuṇḍalinī through the pleasure-way seems very uncertain.

But it is not so, for we can consciously use the pleasure technique of intensity in awakening Kuṇḍalinī in a spontaneous or what we have called the Fusion-way. There are practical steps which simultaneously induce Kuṇḍalinī to arise under the influence of tremendous intensity of rapture and bliss, and at the same time initiate effective measures for the intensification of the brain-potential. This is the method of Awareness with Attention. We saw while discussing the question of Relaxation that the principle to be observed there must be Awareness without Attention — it is a sensorial awareness without cerebral attention. But in the task of intensifying the brain-potential and the releasing of Kuṇḍalinī through intensity arising from pleasure, the principle to be followed is Awareness with Attention. This implies sensorial awareness and cerebral attention. One may put this principle in a different way and say that it is Recognition without Identification. The recognition comes from the brain, but the identification is given by the mind. To recognise but not identify is the surest way to the increasing of the brain potential. To recognise something is to see the fact of that thing; but to identify it is to put it in the framework of psychological memory and then see it. To recognise is to see the picture without a frame, but to identify is to see the picture within the frame supplied by the mind through its memory.

The question is : How to consciously employ the pleasure-technique for the awakening of Kuṇḍalinī and for the increasing of brain-potential ? One can choose a subject of one's intrinsic interest — it may be music, painting, philosophy, mechanics or anything. Since it is a subject of one's own interest there can be no compulsion in its pursuit. If for about half-an-hour one could get completely lost in it, where there is enjoyment but no indulgence, then one will find that this experience greatly helps in arousing intensity. One must enjoy this pursuit without let or hindrance, abandoning oneself in it, so that for that period of enjoyment nothing else exists. This enjoyment must be total so that thought does not enter its field. If thought enters then the experience would be fragmented into the enjoyer and the enjoyed. With this division indulgence is bound to come in. Since it is a pursuit of one's primary interest there could be no question of being distracted by any outer circumstance. One can get lost in it. But a distraction caused by the entry of thought cannot be ruled out. It is possible that one may start identifying with what one is experiencing. This identification means comparison, and therefore judgment is based on that comparison. When this happens then the intensity of enjoyment is lost. Then in the sphere of enjoyment the enjoyer enters. In this enjoyment without the enjoyer there is just the listening or acting without the listener or the actor. If there remains only the listening without the listener then the experience has a wholeness about it, for, it is without the fragmentation caused by a duality. In the ancient book of Kashmir Śaivism, *Vijñāna Bhairava* there is a sūtra which says :

> When eating or drinking, become the taste of the food or drink, and be filled.

To become the taste without the entity who tastes — it is this which is enjoyment without the enjoyer. In this enjoyment there is a great intensity of experience. And this intensity initiates the movement from the sensual to the sensuous. To enjoy the subject of one's intrinsic interest with complete abandonment, and without indulgence, is the secret of awakening through that experience an intensity which is untouched by the enjoyer. Not to have indulgence, and yet be completely abandoned in it, implies that one can end that experience at any moment while one is at the peak of enjoyment. This ending is completely without any resentment or without any lingering look. It is the enjoyer who does not allow such intense experience to end. He demands more and still more of it. But without the enjoyer the experience is complete every moment, and so the question of having more has no relevance whatsoever. One can spend half-an-hour, may be one hour, in this experience of total abandonment with reference to the subject of one's intrinsic interest. In this there can be no question of having a little more extension of time. The demand for time-extension is made by the enjoyer who has corrupted the experience by his act of indulgence. If there is a total abandonment in the act of enjoyment then from it is extracted Pure Intensity — not intensity about anything but just Intensity which moves on to joy and delight, to rapture and bliss and finally to ecstasy. It is the intensity that moves and functions, and, so, as it moves it grows into greater and greater intensity. The sense impacts of such an experience pour this intensity into the cavity of the brain — the un-used portion of this instrument of adaptation which man has and which he must use if he is to solve successfully the problem of his own survival.

While this Intensity pours into the brain, it also awakens the sleeping Kuṇḍalinī. The intensity induces Śakti to draw closer to Śiva. It is only in intensity that the fusion of the two is possible. And the intensity is supplied by that total enjoyment without the presence of the enjoyer. We have seen that the enjoyer is the mind. How to keep out the mind ? How to see that thought does not enter ? When the intensity has touched the brain and activised it, this active brain itself prevents the entry of thought. It is the passive brain which invites the mind with open arms. But an active mind, working under great intensity supplied by the enjoyment left untouched by indulgence, does not allow the mind or the thought process to enter. The brain brooks no interference by the mind while it is engaged in its own legitimate work of giving form and shape to the sensations that pour into the brain from the centres of intense enjoyment. It is our common experience that when we are prone to be caught in an accident, or when we are, for example, crossing a busy road, the brain wants to be left free to make its own calculations without the intrusion by the mind. The brain knows that mind's intrusion at that moment would make its calculations defective with the result that the accident which it has been trying to avoid is bound to overtake the person.

The Human Brain is like a computer, and like all computers it insists that it be fed by correct, full and uncoloured information. The intensity of experience gives the brain-computer full facts, unaltered by the enjoyer or by the process of indulgence. When the brain is fed by more and more sense reports, it has to be tremendously active. It has to bring in more and more areas under the plough. More and more reverberating centres must be opened to process the ever-increasing reports that arrive because of the intensity of experience. It is to this greatly activised brain that the awakened Kuṇḍalinī comes.

The activised brain denotes the masculine energy at its highest. It is to this that the feminine energy of Kuṇḍalinī comes. This is as it should be. It is to the masculine energy working at its highest that the feminine energy of the Kuṇḍalinī must come — for only then is the union of the two perfect. Thus the intensity of enjoyment initiated by pleasure, serves a twofold purpose. One to awaken Kuṇḍalinī under the impact of intensity, and second, to intensify the brain-potential so that more and more of the un-used field is brought under the plough. And this can be done as one enjoys with the totality of cerebral attention any event or happening or object in which one is intrinsically interested. But for this enjoyment thought must not enter, for, it is thought which is the begetter of indulgence. But can thought be prevented from entering the field of enjoyment ? It is interesting to note that thought is always shy. The moment one observes its arrival it disappears. And so in the midst of enjoyment if one is observant of the arrival of thought then it will no longer intrude upon the field of enjoyment. To be completely absorbed in the subject of intrinsic interest, and yet so alert as to step out of that enjoyment any moment, without the slightest hesitation, before it tends to move along the path of indulgence — this is indeed the pleasure way or the fusion way of awakening Kuṇḍalinī and intensifying the brain potential at the same time. In this method the brain is not thrown off its balance as is the case in traditional methods because the brain gets adjusted to the new situation posed by the awakening of Kuṇḍalinī. The adaptation by the brain goes on simultaneously with the receiving of energy through Kuṇḍalinī-awakening. The non-intervention of thought in the moment of enjoyment makes the Brain extra-ordinarily alert. It is able to manifest its masculine nature to the full.

And it is in this state that the **Brain** receives the feminine force of Kuṇḍalinī. Naturally a great amount of new energy is releas-ed with the union of the positive and the negative, the masculine and the negative. This is the fusion or the spontaneous way of awakening Kuṇḍalinī. There are other matters involved in the release of energy but we shall turn to them towards the end of this chapter.

With regard to the question of Kuṇḍalinī that we are consider-ing *vis-a-vis* the human brain, there are three main issues involved. One, the release of energy, second, the prevention of energy-dissipation, and third, the directing an upward movement for the released energy. We shall consider the last point little later. At this stage we are concerned with the first and the second issues. The release of energy should take place when the brain has been activised. It is no longer in a passive condition. This activising of the brain is necessary if it is to receive the energy released by the awakening of Kuṇḍalinī. It is this point which is missed in the traditional Haṭha Yoga practices. If the Kuṇḍa-linī energy reaches the brain while it is in a dull and a passive state, then the extra energy will create an unbalancing of the brain. The passive brain would not know what to do with the extra energy. It is because of this that through enjoyment with-out indulgence the brain must be activised. It will get activised because the entry of thought in the moment of enjoyment will not take place. It is the entry of thought in the midst of ex-periencing that renders the brain passive. But when thought does not enter, the brain will be induced to work on the sensa-tions received in moments of full undistracted enjoyment. Not only will the brain be activised, the senses too will be rendered more responsive to the outer impacts of life. Thus in the con-dition of an alert brain and the sensitivised senses, if the Kuṇḍa-linī energy enters the brain, it will find a ready union with the brain that has been properly prepared. Then the new energy will be utilised by the brain to open numerous new centres of learning.

We have so far considered only the question of Intensity. We must turn to the question of Variety as it forms an important link in the chain of intensifying the brain potential. We have seen that when indulgence is not allowed to enter the experience of pleasure then intensity of enjoyment grows and there comes into being a movement from the sensual to the sensuous. This question of intensity has been stated in one of the sutras of *Vijñāna Bhairava* thus :

> Keep attentive on the fire in the beginning, and
> so continuing avoid the embers in the end.

The above statement says that the fire must remain alive upto the end so much so that even at the end it must not peter out into smouldering ashes. The intensity must not get slowed down, but this is possible only when there is enjoyment without the enjoyer. While this deals with the problem of Intensity, there still remains the question of Variety. In Intensity the brain will be activised so that from a passive state it comes to an active condition. In this active condition when it receives the Kuṇḍalinī energy, released in such moments of unflagging intensity, there must come into active operation new centres of learning. In other words, there must take place the intensification of the brain-potential so that barren parts of the brain may get fertilized due to the fresh waters available for the irrigation of unused fields. It is this which calls forth consideration of the question of Variety.

While for Intensity it is the subject of intrinsic interest that needs to be invoked, for Variety one has to choose some subject, or subjects of secondary interest. The more the subjects of secondary interest, the greater is the variety that is available to the brain to work upon. Unfortunately most of us have neither absorbing intrinsic interests nor variety of secondary interests. In the working of the brain under such conditions there are only grooves formed, and so one goes on with monotonous movements along those beaten tracks which produce boredom and tiredness. The brain must be taken out of the grooves, from the monotony of the beaten track. It is true that in the subject of secondary interest one cannot so easily be absorbed as in the subject of intrinsic interest. But with a little effort an interest can be aroused. In the beginning it would be good to select the subject of secondary interest which is as close to the subject of intrinsic interest as possible. But gradually one must move further and further away so that the secondary interest belongs to a category completely different from the subject of intrinsic or primary interest. It is only thus that variety can be built up. When the brain has been activised and when intensity has released Kundalinī-energy, the impacts coming from the areas of secondary interest will bring into existence new reverberating centres of learning. But with regard to the secondary interest, the same principles of Awareness with Attention, and Enjoyment without Indulgence must be rigorously followed. Here the entry of thought is more likely, but one can prevent it by observing the arrival of thought. In the subject of secondary interest, to observe the arrival of thought will be easy. When the thought finds no entry, enjoyment without indulgence in the sphere of secondary interest will cause no difficulty. If one can experiment daily both with subjects of intrinsic interest as well as the subject of secondary interest then the brain will not only be activised, but will be able to use the energy coming from Kuṇḍalinī awakening for bringing more and more areas of its unused fields under the plough. Intensity and Variety will bring the whole of the brain into active condition, so that, not merely ten per cent of the brain potential but the full potential of the brain will be brought under active operation. It goes without saying that the pursuit of secondary interest also must have its initial start in pleasure without indulgence as otherwise it will become a factor contributing to the dissipation of energy released under conditions of intensity. In the secondary interest also the movement must start from the sensual to the sensuous so that it also adds to the energy-release based on its own intensity, although subdued in nature.

But one may say that if one's life is full of unmitigated suffering and unrelieved pain, how can one use the pleasure-technique for Kuṇḍalinī-awakening and for intensifying the brain-potential ? When there are no moments of pleasure, what is one to do ? Should one get resigned to one's plight or can one employ the expansion-technique of pleasure as against the contraction-technique of pain ? Such a person too can move along the fusion-way. If in the present circumstances of such a person there are no incidents of pleasure, then he can recover past events of joy through his memory. He can re-live those events and happenings; but with the same approach as we have discussed, namely, enjoyment without indulgence. This re-living in memory must not degenerate into day-dreaming. The purpose of re-living through memory the happy moments of the past is only to awaken intensity, and not to seek an escape from the unhappy conditions of the present. Such re-living can be for a short duration, ten to fifteen minutes at a time. But if the memory-re-living is vivid and strong then it will not be different from such an experience in the present. Such vivid re-living in memory will call out intensity which once again will move from the sensual to the sensuous. In such movement intensity will grow and serve the twofold purpose of activising the brain and releasing the Kuṇḍalinī energy. With memory, one can experiment both in terms of subjects of intrinsic interest and the subjects of secondary interest. Surely one can recollect such events and happenings from the past, and thus employ the pleasure-technique for the intensification of the brain-potential. As we have stated earlier our aim at Kuṇḍalinī awakening is only for intensifying the brain-potential so that the Brain can effectively and efficiently deal with the challenges of life.

It is hardly necessary to point out that what can be done with the help of Memory can also be done with Imagination. One can vividly imagine events and happenings of pleasure. And the vividness of imagination will once again be as good as actual happenings. This will release intensity, and if indulgence is not allowed to enter, then this intensity will grow in greater intensity initiating a movement towards joy and delight, rapture and bliss and finally to the experience of ecstasy. Thus the pleasure-without-indulgence technique can be available to all, the fortunate and the seemingly unfortunate ones too.

This is the spontaneous way of intensifying the brain potential and, for that purpose releasing the Kuṇḍalinī energy. The spontaneous way is the safe way, firstly because it can be practised by any individual without the need for a guru or an expert. Secondly it is safe because it prepares the brain to receive the Kuṇḍalinī energy by first making it active even within the confines of its existing potential. A dull and a passive brain can ill-afford to have the flow of energy arriving from Kuṇḍalinī. And so, in the fusion way, which we have been discussing, there is the unfailing safety measure of preparing the brain through the shedding of its dullness and passivity. It has also to be remembered that in this fusion-way we are not concerned with the activising of various Cakras through āsanas and concentration. Along this way the Kuṇḍalinī force moves on to the cavity of the Brain where with the meeting of the negative and the positive poles a new energy is released. This is indeed the union of Śiva and Śakti. From such union of Love is born energy most potent and powerful. Then Kuṇḍalinī Śakti descends, and in its descent activises the various Cakras. The stimulation of the Cakras is done by energy itself. With the descent of Kuṇḍalinī to the Mūlādhāra centre there takes place again its fresh ascent under intensity. The ascent and descent of Kuṇḍalinī becomes a rhythm which maintains the biological mechanism in conditions of health and vigour. It is a mistaken idea that Kuṇḍalinī is aroused once for all and then the spiritual aspirant can sit back in his easy chair. The flow of Kuṇḍalinī has to be constant so that the human brain receives fresh energy from time to time for the discharge of its arduous duties. In each ascent and descent the various Cakras get more and more vivified, but in a natural and an effortless manner. It is not we who vivify the Cakras, it is Kuṇḍalinī energy itself that does it as it descends after re-vitalising the brain.

In all discussions of Kuṇḍalinī-awakening there is one word which is constantly mentioned, and which is regarded as the key-word. This is *Ūrdhva-retas* or the upward movement of energy. In the traditional literature on Kuṇḍalinī this is interpreted as the upward movement of the sex-energy. Such interpretation has become prevalent because the wider meaning of the word *Retas* has not been taken into account. *Retas* does not mean merely the seminal energy. One of the meanings of the word *Retas* is *Dhārā* meaning flow of current. Thus *Retas* implies flow of energy, including the sex-energy, but not exclusively sex-energy. The biological energy may be released due to the intensity of pleasure. And as we have seen this intensity grows more and more and there is a movement from the sensual to the sensuous. This energy released under the impact of intensity must be turned upwards for thus alone the brain can be benefited by it. If it flows downwards then the energy is bound to get dissipated. How is this energy to be turned upwards ? There is only one way, and it is by simple practices of *Prāṇāyāma.* The energy released is itself a vital energy, rejuvenating the biological mechanism. Since it is vital energy it is through the help of the vital breath or *Prāṇa* that its upward movement can become possible. This Prāṇāyāma practice is not such as would need the presence of a guru or an expert teacher. It is known as *Bhastrikā Prāṇāyāma.* It is described in the *Haṭhayogapradīpikā* as follows :

> Bhastrikā should be thus performed : Press the left nostril with the ring and little finger and by the right nostril inhale and exhale like a pair of bellows. When tired, perform Kumbhaka inhaling by the right nostril and exhaling by the left. Then press the right nostril and, inhale and exhale like the bellows through the left nostril etc. Thus go on alternately till tired. This is one method.
>
> The other way of practising it is to close the left nostril, and inhale as much as possible by the right nostril, quickly close that nostril and then exhale gradually through the left nostril. This should be done many times.

There is an alternative to the second method also which says that the exhaling should also be done as quick and as deep as the inhaling. And so we have three main methods for the performance of the Bhastrikā Prāṇāyāma. It is quite simple and does not require the presence of any expert or experienced teacher. One can do this by oneself without any danger whatsoever. However, one must heed one warning — and that is, it should not be overdone. This *Bhastrikā Prāṇāyāma* brings the upward movement of energy into operation naturally and spontaneously. And so the way of fusion is, Intensity for the release of energy, Non-indulgence for preventing the dissipation of energy, and Bhastrikā Prāṇāyāma for the turning upwards of the released energy so as to revitalise the Human brain enabling it to function with greater and greater potential.

We have discussed the question of Brain-potential at great length because it is the crux of the matter so far as Meditation is concerned. It is by it alone that the bridge connecting the Body with the Mind will be strengthened. In this age of fast moving tempo of life we need a Brain which can adapt itself quickly and efficiently to the needs posed by the challenges of life. If man is to survive biologically and psychologically then the birth of such a Brain and the emergence of a New Mind are absolutely necessary. In this chapter we have discussed the birth of the re-vitalised Brain due to the inflow of the Kuṇḍalinī energy aroused in the intensity of joy. This Brain must be integrated so that the masculine and the feminine counterparts function together. This integration demands the Union of Śiva and Śakti. Without the inflow of the Kuṇḍalinī Sakti the brain functions only in its masculine aspect. When Śakti rushes to meet Śiva then in their close embrace takes place the fusion of the negative and the positive, of the masculine and the feminine. In this fusion comes into being the re-vitalisation of the brain and the rejuvenation of the entire body.

But such a Brain has its own problems of establishing perfect order within its new and enlarged campus, and initiating lines of efficient communication between Brain and the world around. It is to these problems that we shall turn in the subsequent pages.

NINE

ORDER AND SPACE

J. KRISHNAMURTI, one of the most eminent and the revolutionary thinkers of our age says in his book *The Urgency of Change* :

> The brain cannot stand disorder. If there is disorder all its activities will be contradictory, confused, miserable and it will bring about mischief in itself and around itself. It is disorder in the brain that brings about conflict.

One may ask : From where does disorder arise in the brain ? And what is the nature of its conflict? For this one has to understand the constitution of the Human Brain. We have already stated in the earlier part of the book that broadly there are two divisions of the Brain — one, the Old Brain, and, the other, the New Brain. The Old brain is the legacy of our animal existence and so contains animal propensities with powerful emotional urges. The New Brain or the Cortex belongs to the human individual and is growing with the evolutionary growth of man. Compared to the Old Brain the New Brain is an infant. The relationship between the two is one of the major problems in man's cerebral activities. The Old Brain is used to quick responses. It is made up of reflex actions. When an animal is hungry, it cannot wait, it must see that the hunger is satisfied immediately. But a human individual, when hungry, can delay the processes of satisfying his hunger. The Cortex which is specially Human is like a moderator. It wishes to calculate and then act, whereas the animal brain cannot afford to wait. It can brook no delay. John Pfeiffer says in his book *The Human Brain* :

> The cortex is a bit of a professor, slightly on the academic side. Left to itself it would speculate endlessly . . . . Most of the time the old brain nags the Cortex into useful activity. It says "Hurry, here is my problem, analyse it and report back within a minute". The cortex replies "Now that is an extremely interesting problem. It may have some implications you haven't explored thoroughly. I must look into them. It reminds me of . . . . " "Hurry within a minute" interrupts the old brain.

The problems of relationship between the Old Brain and the Cortex are immense. It is out of these problems of relationship that conflict and disorder arise. Bruce Bliven says :

> We must try to keep the old brain and the new in proper proportion to each other, remembering that when either gets the upper hand too completely the human being cannot properly fulfil his destiny.

In cases of brain disorder sometimes surgeons, performing frontal lobotomy, an operation which becomes necessary under acute conditions, cut out the fibers connecting the Old and the New Brain so as to end the conflict between the two. But this is only a palliative, for, it cannot cure the problem of relationship between the two. The state of perfect order in the brain demands a harmonious relationship between the Human and the Animal parts of the brain. A continuous conflict between the two impairs greatly the functioning of the brain.

Ordinarily our brain functions under conditions of disorder and disharmony. This is evident from the way we do our normal things of life. The disorder of the brain is exhibited in the disorderly way in which we perform our actions or the way in which we meet the situations of life. Very often we say our memory is defective. Nobody's memory is defective unless some serious damage has been caused to the brain. The brain is the repository of factual memory even as mind is the repository of psychological memory. Scientists have experimented by inserting electrical devices in the memory centre of the brain, and they have found that the brain retains fully its memory content ; even the events and the happenings of the earliest years are recorded by the brain and kept in tact. It is not our memory that is defective. It is true that we do not remember certain things, and can recall them only after a great effort. What happens in such cases is defective observation or defective hearing. When we hear during periods of brain's disorder, then our hearing is bound to be defective. If that is so, how can we remember aright what has been said. In such states of disorder the brain has been wool-gathering, or, in simple terms, we have been absent-minded. In such wool-gathering it is obvious that what comes to the brain from the senses is not received by the brain completely. This is due to the fact that the relationship between the Cortex and the Old Brain is far from satisfactory. The attention of the Cortex is diverted elsewhere, and so even though we see, we do not see, even though we hear, we do not hear. The brain being a computer needs to be fed properly. But when it is wool-gathering such feeding becomes impossible. Surely the brain should be helped to restore order. This means it should be encouraged to establish right relationship between its two components. How is this to be done ?

One must see first how one is actually disorderly in one's behaviour. Unless this disorder is clearly perceived it will be impossible to help the brain to come to a state of order and sanity. Usually our belongings are in a pell-mell condition. We are not even aware of the way in which the physical objects of our life are lying — leave apart the disorder in which our ideas and thoughts are. Our physical existence is like living in a godown and that too a disorderly godown. Due to this prevailing disorder we are unable to use our time and energy in an orderly manner. We complain about time, but we do not realize that the lack of time largely is felt because we do not know how to organise the time at our disposal in an orderly manner. It is said that Lord Baden Powell, the founder of the Scout Movement, when he came to India, was in search of a proper person who would organise Scout movement in India in an efficient manner. Some one suggested to him the name of Dr. Annie Besant, but he was told that Dr. Besant was the busiest person in India. On hearing this, Lord Baden Powell seems to have remarked: "If she is the busiest person then she is the right person for it is the busiest person who can find time for more work." It is because we do not know how to organise our time that we complain about the lack of time. Here one sees the brain in a state of disorder. Such a brain is lazy and indolent, content to wallow in conditions that are far from satisfactory. Such a brain gets accustomed to anything, even to the most abject disorder in one's environment. This is what has happened to most of us.

We find that in our office and home surroundings we rarely bring about any changes in the physical pattern of things. Things are kept in the same place for years and years. The brain and the senses get used to this state, and therefore one does not feel any necessity to change things or to rearrange them. In order to induce the brain to come to a state of order, it is always helpful to change the arrangements of things, of furniture, of books, or of anything, from time to time. By this rearrangement we will find that the same room with the same furniture looks different. A certain amount of freshness is imparted to it. The brain is induced to take more interest in it. The brain feels energetic by this simple act of re-arranging one's outer environment. There comes a little more pleasure to live in the newly arranged room.

When there is a state of order, at any level, there is bound to be an experience of increased space. In fact, order creates space. The brain gets congested when it cannot function in a state of order. Such congestion brings confusion into existence. When one brings about a re-arrangement in one's outer environment, from time to time, then the brain feels more space in its own functioning area. With the creation of order, space too is created, resulting in easier movement. To re-arrange one's outer environment seems so simple that one does not associate it with meditation or spiritual life. But we do not realize that where order and space are not there happens a great deal of wastage of one's time, one's energies and one's resources too. In a state of disorder the Old Brain has its ascendency over the New Brain. In this condition the Cortex becomes subservient to the demands and urges of the Old Brain. In the very simple act of re-arranging one's outer environment the Cortex is able to maintain its balance against the upsurge of the Old Brain. The outer order created by such re-arrangement helps the brain to function with a great sense of order.

The Old and the New Brain are very delicately balanced. Even the slightest thing disturbs the balance putting the brain-machinery out of gear. John Pfeiffer has expressed this fact in a clear manner in his book *The Human Brain*. He says :

> Most long-lived species that are with us today represent evolutionary dead-ends. Some of them found their niches, settled down and have reproduced practically unchanged for as much as 400,000,000 years. The tendency is strong in even the most highly advanced animals. Give a chimpanzee, a few chimpanzees, a peaceful stretch of jungle and plenty of bananas, and it will live happily for the rest of its life. Give a man an environment correspondingly idyllic, say a Garden of Eden, and he will get into trouble. Getting into trouble is our genius and glory as a species. Of all animals we are the only ones with brain sufficiently complex to keep us in a constant state of "maladjustment".

It is needless to say that the cause of this maladjustment is the conflict between the Cortex and the Old Brain. This conflict is evidenced most clearly in the Dream phenomena. Dream is a very complex phenomenon, for, there are numerous causes that induce dreams. During one night's sleep it is said that we dream at least three times with certain intervals. It has been found that during the dream condition, even though the person is asleep, his eye-balls move as if he is seeing something. The movement of the eye-balls denotes that in the dream condition the brain is active.

From the nature of the movement of the eye-balls, the intensity or non-intensity of the dream is being measured. As stated above dreams are caused by various factors. There are dreams which are caused by some physical constriction or by the mind desiring to fulfil un-fulfilled desires, or the dream may be an actual out-of-the-body experience. There is vast literature dealing with dreams and dream-interpretations. Truly speaking dreams cannot be interpreted by another person as he would not know all the facts comprising a dream. But the dream cannot be interpreted even by the person himself. The dreamer and the dream are not different. They are related as the observer and the observed. The observed has no independent existence apart from the observer. Similarly dream has no independent existence apart from the dreamer. How can the dreamer interpret his own dream. If he does, it would be a coloured or prejudiced interpretation. Dream is not a problem, it is the dreamer that constitutes a problem. And without understanding the dreamer any interpretation of dream would be meaningless.

Apart from the above categories of dreams, the one main category is that which is caused by the condition of the brain. If brain is active during moments of dream, as evidenced by the movement of the eye-balls, then surely it is fully involved in it. By and large, it is the situation prevailing in the brain that determines the nature of the dream. The state of dream indicates the desire of one part of the brain to communicate with the other. For such communication, dream is the best avenue. During the night's sleep this communication goes on, as during the waking hours such communication between the Cortex and the Old Brain is well-nigh impossible. The conflicts between the New and the Old Brain find release during the dream-communication. When we wake up in the morning we have no clear idea of the nature of dream we have had. All the three or more dreams get overlapped and we get a confused picture when we wake up. Sometimes we wake up in the middle of the dream. If during waking hours there could be sane and healthy communication between the Old and the New Brain then we would be free from the disturbance of dreams during the night's sleep. The disorder prevailing in the brain due to conflict, projects itself in the dream. If the brain could be brought to a condition of order then we could enjoy sound sleep. How to bring this order so that we may be free from the dream-disturbance? Or to put it differently, how to get order restored in the brain through the stoppage of disturbing dreams? J. Krishnamurti says in his book *The Urgency of Change*:

> It can be done through watchfulness during the day, and then before sleeping, by putting everything that has been done during the day in order. In that way the brain does not go to sleep in disorder. This does not mean that the brain hypnotises itself into a state of order when there is really disorder in and about it. There must be order during the day, and the summing up of this order before sleeping is the harmonious ending of the day. It is like a man who keeps accounts and balances them properly every evening so that he starts afresh the next day.

Krishnamurti here suggests the Way of Review before going to sleep. It is not Review that by itself will solve all problems, but it is an additional instrument which can be employed so that during the hours of sleep the brain enjoys a state of order and its energies do not get frittered away. This review will be first superficial in its nature, meaning it will be a review of the incidents and events through which one has passed during the day. The purpose of such a review is to arrange the day's events neatly and tidily, one by one, so that they do not overlap but maintain their proper sequence. It is like closing the accounts for the day with no loose ends left unattended. The superficial aspect of the review is to pass through the events and happenings of the day. When this is done then one can review one's reactions and responses to those events and happenings. But in this process of review two things have to be observed. One, the review must be backwards, and not forwards. One must go from the night to the morning backwards, and not from the morning to the night forward. The second thing to be observed is that while reviewing there must be no judgment of what happened and how one reacted, no act of repentance, and no resolve for the next day, saying that one will avoid certain things, and one will pursue certain other things. It must be a pure review with no judgment or evaluation. Due to this review the brain will be able to experience a sense of order, and, so, while we are asleep it will not have to struggle to establish order within its campus. It is this struggle of the brain during our sleep hours that produces disturbing and sometimes night-marish dreams. It is hardly necessary to say that under these conditions we will be able to sleep soundly, and the brain too will be able to rest. We are bound to arise in the morning refreshed with the brain working under conditions of perfect order, and therefore efficiently. As we have stated this review must be without any sense of regret or repentance, and without any resolve to behave better the next day. A review forwards always puts the brain into activity, but a review backwards, as suggested above, will keep the brain comparatively quiet. It is only in such quietness that order can be easily established. And so along with the re-arrangement of outer environment, consisting of things and objects, if one could experiment with the review of events and also one's react ons then one will be able to help the brain to come to a state of order which is necessary for its efficient functioning.

Most of us have memories which are shaky and therefore undependable. We are referring to factual memory, and not psychological memory. The brain is the rapository of factual memory. But as stated above when we look back we find that our facts are mostly unreliable. With regard to subjects of great emotional involvement the facts are covered over with psychological super-impositions. But that is not all. Memories with regard to non-psychological matters are also very shaky because our perceptions of those things themselves were casual. We will not go into the questions raised by psychological memory as that is outside the purview of the Brain. But for our sane and healthy living our factual memory must be sound and perfectly reliable. This confusion in factual memory is one of the major causes leading to disorder in the functioning of the brain. A brain in a state of perfect order is most precise in the memory of facts.

One of the most effective ways of restoring order in the functioning of the brain is the restructuring of memory. By restructuring we mean, putting the memory of facts in perfect sequential order. It is the sequence of facts that is shaky with most of us. One can take up various events and happenings of life and start restructuring the memory-sequence with regard to them. When an attempt is made towards restructuring then one will find that one begins to remember great many small details. Such restructuring should be started with regard to events and happenings that have left a mark on our memory. When this is done, one can turn to events and happenings which have been casual and of no special importance. With regard to the restructuring of memory one can go over the same events, or group of events, again and again so that no detail is missed, and all facts are put in perfect sequential order. This will be a great relief to the brain, for, it will be able to function with a great sense of order and harmony.

In the restructuring of memory we are concerned with the sequential order of a number of associative happenings in which singular events are likely to remain out of focus. In so doing some aspects of memory are bound to remain confused and hazy. This evidently contributes to a state of disorder in the brain. And so along with the restructuring of sequential memory there should also be the Re-call of singular memory — that is, memory of single episodes in the midst of sequential association of events. Usually while we are able to remember a large number of associated happenings, we are unable to immediately recall a single detail out of them. To remember things in the process of association is easy, but a sudden recall of some detail is extremely difficult. But a brain that is in a state of perfect order should not find it difficult to recall a particular fact from among a large number of other facts. If one experiments with the recall of singular facts one will find that thereby the brain is considerably helped in its work of restoring order within its functioning campus. It does not matter how small is the event comprising the singular memory. The greater the recall of very small details the greater is the order and efficiency restored to the brain. It is hardly necessary to point out that both the Restructuring and the Recall will serve as memory-training which will stand one in good stead with reference to the challenges and impacts of life. An alert brain must be precise in the sphere of factual memory, and this precision itself will keep back the intrusion of psychological memory.

The four devices mentioned in this chapter — namely, Rearrangement of outer environment, Review of the day's happening without judgment or resolve, Restructuring of the sequential memory of facts, and the Recall of singular details in the midst of a group of events — will go a long way in enabling the brain to function with perfect order. These devices will strengthen the capacities of the Cortex so that it is not overwhelmed by the inroads of the Old Brain. In the struggle between the Old and the New Brain, it is the latter which is at a disadvantage at present due to its comparative infancy. With the strengthening of the Cortex by the devices suggested here, a balance will be established between the Old and the New Brain. Released from conflicts, the Brain will be able to function with great efficiency.

While the establishment of order within the campus of the Brain is essential, and particularly so in the background of the inflow of Kuṇḍalinī energy, it has also to be remembered that the Brain must be able to communicate with the outer world and that too with great effectiveness. If its capacity to communicate does not increase then the intensifying of the brain potential will have very little value. The contacts of the Brain with the outside world must be limitless and this must be both with regard to its receptivity as well as its capacity of communication. And so we shall turn to the problem of communication with reference to the New Brain in the next chapter.

TEN

NEAR AND YET FAR

IT is a strange paradox of our age that while we have evolved most sophisticated media of mass communication, there is hardly any communication between individuals. Our instruments of communication in this civilization are excellent for social and collective purposes. But, by and large, when two individuals meet there is very little to communicate, and, more than that, there are no effective means for such communication. Physically near but psychologically far apart — this is the peculiar phenomenon that we see today everywhere. In the matter of communication there are two main questions : What to communicate ? and How to communicate ? The first question has relevance with the Mind, but the second has to do with the Brain. In this age of tremendous developments in almost all spheres of life, it is obvious that the Mind has much to convey. But the Human Brain has no adequate technique to communicate what the mind conveys. The content of communication obviously belongs to the Mind, but the technique of communication, at the physical level, is certainly the province of the Brain.

It is in the sphere of communication that one realises the most, the inadequacy of the functioning capacity of our brain as it is constituted today. Its low potential is a great drawback in communicating at the physical level what is conveyed by the mind. At the individual level we find that people are moving more and more apart for lack of communication. It is true that Communication can be effective only in the background of Communion. And modern man has become almost a stranger to the experience of communion. The subject of communion very largely belongs to the Mind. And therefore the question of Communication brings us to the very threshold of the Mind. We said that communion is very largely the province of the Mind. We say, largely, because there are fields of communion at the brain-level too. We have discussed this in the previous chapters in terms of Awareness with Attention but without Identification. It is in this process that we come to communion where the senses and the brain experience with a totality of attention, and without the interference from the mind, events and happenings at the physical level, be they the listening of music, the witnessing of the grandeur of nature, be it the performance of action or anything else lying within the range of the five senses. This experience of communion increases the brain-potential so that it is able to pick up more and more of the messages and instructions of the Mind. But while it is one thing to pick up these messages, it is something entirely different to put them in effective communication channels. The Brain must be powerful and alert enough to receive the instructions of the mind, and this is what is sought to be done by the intensification of the brain-potential, a subject which we have discussed at great length in the earlier chapters. The brain-potential increases as a result of communion at the level of the senses and the brain. But even when this is done, the question of establishing communication links with the outer world, at the physical level, remains. And without this, the awakening of Kuṇḍalinī and the intensification of the brain-potential lose all their meaning. The brain, functioning as a bridge, must not only receive the increased load coming from the mind but it must carry it to the other end. If there is no clear passage of this traffic across the bridge, then there is bound to be congestion and confusion on the bridge itself. This will impair the functioning of the brain in a very serious manner. And so the problem of communication is as important as the three major problems of the brain which we have so far considered, namely, Relaxation, Intensification and Orderliness. All these must be for the purposes of effective Communication.

It is not difficult to realise that our communication is far from satisfactory. We may read a lot but we are unable to communicate what we have read to others in an intelligible manner. We may hear lectures and talks but we cannot effectively convey to others what we have heard. We may listen to music and enjoy very much such listening, and yet we are unable to pass on that joy to others in a manner that makes them also participants in our joy, once again in an intelligent manner. Effective communication at any level, demands a linking up with the level of another. We may soar to great heights but we are unable to bring the experience of that enjoyment to those who cannot rise to our heights. We may be great scholars but we are unable to speak in the language of the students. Great prophets and thinkers have always spoken of the highest things in the simplest language. The saints and the mystics of all ages and of all countries have conveyed their noblest experiences in a language that even the most illiterate have been able to understand. Usually we communicate with others in a pedantic language where there is more a show of words than the simple and intelligent way of conveying what one alleges to have understood. But such simple and intelligent communication depends on one's experiences of communion and also on the clear and effective channels of communication that one has evolved.

By and large, when two individuals meet they talk shop. Our communication with each other moves in a groove. We are unable to establish a rapport with the other person. And it is this which is the main cause of distorted human relationships which we see everywhere. When the brain is greatly energised with the inflow of Kuṇḍalinī force it needs very powerful means of communication. And if these are not available then the brain feels all the more frustrated. And so in the context of what we have discussed, in the course of our comprehensive inquiry into the subject of Meditation, this question of Communication assumes a great importance. Communion alone will not solve our problem. There have been mystics and saints who have come to deep and profound experiences of Communion but in the absence of effective means of communication they have felt utterly frustrated so much so that in this frustration they have behaved in an abnormal manner.

But the question is : How to build effective channels of communication which the brain can use not only for expressing its own experiences of communion, but also for conveying instructions and experiences of the mind as well ? Man is a social animal which means he is an animal that communicates with other members of the species. But other animals and birds also communicate with each other. While this is true, their range of communication is very small. They use sounds and gestures to convey their experiences with each other. It is man alone who has evolved an intricate language system for the communication of his ideas, his feelings and his experiences to others. Even language itself has been evolved from mere sounds and words to something that is amazing for conveying subtle and intangible ideas and feelings to other members of the human race. Man too employs gestures and symbols where even words fail — but this is because his experiences are of such a nature that no language can convey them adequately. In fact, even words forming a language are symbols, and there is no end to the evolution of more and more word-symbols. Communication becomes a problem to man as it does not seem to become among birds and animals. He has therefore to go on perfecting his means of communications, not merely in a generalised and collective sphere, but between individuals. It is not the question of perfecting merely the mechanical techniques of communication, what is needed is the perfection of communication between human beings, not just between groups of human individuals. What conscious efforts can be made to perfect the ways of communication so as to bring human beings together in bonds of greater understanding ?

Unfortunately one has never seriously applied one's mind to this problem. Our communication with others is either by written word or by spoken word or by gestures which constitute symbolical language to be used where language of words seems to fail. Even the language of words has to be supplemented with gestures so as to give necessary emphasis to a particular point which we wish to convey. The human brain has, among other centres, the centre of speech which motivates all acts of articulation. In any process of communication two things are needed — first, the urge to communicate, and second, the capacity to articulate. The urge to communicate is bound to arise with the intensification of the brain potential, but if the capacity of right articulation is not there then the added powers of the brain will result in frustration. It is interesting to note that in the *Taittrīya Upaniṣad*, the teacher begins the subject of education with right articulation. This articulation may be in words or it may be in gestures. It is the way of clear and lucid expression. This expression may be in terms of music or dance, in terms of painting or poetry or in terms of speaking and writing. The question is: How to consciously cultivate the technique of articulation or expression which is clear and lucid ? There have been instances when a person has been inspired by something, but having no technique of right expression, the energy released in moments of inspiration has been wasted in things that are unpleasant and unbecoming. Since we have emphasised in the earlier chapters the need for the awakening of Kuṇḍalinī for supplying greater energy to the brain, the question of communication, of right articulation, has assumed special importance. Right communication demands the Art of Attunement and the Science of Articulation. Here we use the word "articulation" in its widest sense, not merely in the sense of voice production and pronunciation. We said in the very beginning of this book that to act rightly is to do the right thing, at the right moment and in the right manner. This is the most appropriate description of real communication. It contains both Attunement as well as Articulation. The Brain that is alert and functioning under full potential is bound to adapt itself to the outer impacts in such a manner that its mode of action displays the right thing at the right time and in the right manner.

But how to train or to induce the Brain, to function through such channels of communication as would result in right action.

In communication of this nature the brain must approximate its modes of expression in such a manner that the communicator is able to reach the person with whom communication is sought to be established, and that too at the level of that person. To be able to meet at the same level, at the same time and with the same intensity is surely the secret of right communication. It matters little what medium of expression one uses. Normally it is through the spoken word or the written word that one communicates with the other. One may not be a public speaker, but one uses the power of speech in formal or informal conversation. One may not write books but one uses the written word in one's letters, personal or otherwise. But most of us are unable to use the power of the spoken and the written word with effectiveness so as to evolve a meaningful communication. Our spoken and written words lack both strength as well as clarity. They are much too vague and feeble to carry any conviction to the other person. Our spoken and written word must have both clarity and intensity. Sometimes we have much to convey, and yet we are unable to convey effectively. When the Brain is surcharged with new energy in the wake of its increased potential, it will be able to learn much more than it does at present. But it is said, and rightly, that we learn best when we teach others what we have learnt. The technique of teaching others is the art and science of communication. Since we have already discussed, and, that too in great detail, how the human brain can establish newer and newer centres of learning, we must now see how this learning can be deepened by perfecting our channels of communication so that we may teach others while we ourselves continue our own learning. The Brain that has stopped learning cannot teach others, that is, it cannot communicate in an effective manner with others. Teach as you learn is the best principle that one can adopt if one is to establish effective channels of communication with the world around.

In all questions of communication two things are essential. One, the capacity to retain what one has experienced, and second, the capacity to pass on one's experience to others in a manner that is most effective. When one is able to experience something without the intervention of thought then the question of retention does not pose a problem. If one's experience has been casual then retention is almost impossible because there is hardly anything to retain! The experiments about which we have spoken in the earlier chapters with reference to enjoyment without indulgence indicate to us clearly the way of retention. Our present inquiry is : How to communicate to others the experiences that have been retained by us ? It would be best for one to experiment first by seeing or listening or experiencing anything with a totality of Awareness and cerebral Attention. Then moving away from that experience one may audibly or inaudibly repeat what one has experienced. In other words, one may verbalize it to oneself what one has seen, heard, read or experienced. This is a question of faithful reproduction to oneself what one may have experienced as far as possible in the language in which we have seen, heard, read or experienced. This is the Technique of Reproduction of what we may have heard, or read, or listened. Whatever we have experienced should be repeated or imitated, audibly or inaudibly, as far as possible in the language or the manner in which we had experienced. This should be as faithful a replica of the original as possible. This will generate in us a sense of confidence in the matter of expression or communication.

When one is able to do this, one can move further, and, that is to reproduce what one has experienced in one's own language and in one's own way. In this, one must completely eschew the language and expression of the author whose book one may have read, or the mannerisms of voice production which one may have heard while listening to music. Here too there is a process of verbalization but it is in one's own language and mannerism. While the content is not original the mode of expression is one's own. In this experiment one is trying to teach to others what one has learnt. This can be done in diverse ways. One can stand in front of an imaginary audience and start talking to it about some simple or abstruse subject but in one's own language. This will be an inaudible articulation, for, one cannot loudly start speaking to an audience that does not exist ! This inaudible articulation in the form of a talk before an imaginary audience will increase one's power of communication a great deal. The same thing can be done with regard to music or whatever other experience one has had. This is the Technique of Adaptation. The earlier technique meant repeating what one had experienced in as faithful a manner as possible. But in this second experiment we use the method of adaptation. There can be a great deal of variety in the modes of expression along the line of adaptation. But both these techniques use the power of the spoken word, audible or inaudible — in fact, mostly inaudible. Such inaudible verbalization in order to reproduce something that one has experienced or to adapt it in terms of one's own modes of expression releases a great deal of the power of effective communication. The greater the variety of adaptation, the greater is the richness in one's ways of expression. That which has been done inaudibly can easily be transferred at the audible level.

The spoken word, however effective it may be, tends to be vague and verbose. It is necessary that one should be clear and precise in one's expressions. In this, the written word is the most appropriate medium. When one writes, one has to be clear if one's writing has to have any value whatsoever. And what we have discussed with reference to the spoken word becomes applicable to the written word as well. This means that one must employ the two techniques — of reproducing what one has experienced and of adaptation in one's own language of what one has seen or heard or read or otherwise experienced. These two practices with reference to the written word will greatly improve our powers of expression and communication.

While reproducing what one has known or experienced and while adapting what one has known or experienced in one's own language and modes of expression it must be realised that they do not exhaust all aspects of communication. Even moving from the spoken to the written word leaves certain aspects of communication untouched. It is necessary that one communicates something of one's own, and not merely of what others have known or experienced. Even in adaptation one is not concerned with one's own experience. And so while practices for reproduction and adaptation are necessary, one must seek for something original, independent or individual. One can start with the spoken word so that audibly or inaudibly one expresses oneself in a somewhat original manner. This brings a creative factor in one's manner of communication. Whether the subject is original or not, its treatment must have something of individuality in it. In communication we are essentially concerned with the treatment of a subject. It would be interesting to do one's own communication on a particular subject, both spoken and written, and then compare our treatment of the subject with others who have also treated the same subject or subjects. We have discussed here the subject of communication only in terms of the spoken and the written word. One can gradually use other media of expression too but in terms of the above threefold technique of Reproduction, of Adaptation, and of Individuation.

While one may evolve and perfect different techniques of communication and it is necessary so to do — in the ultimate analysis, that which is communicated must have a naturalness and spontaneity about it. If this does not happen then what flows through the elaborately planned channels of communication will not be fresh and living. It is the function of the brain to supply perfect channels of communication at the physical level, but the passage of the brain connecting the body with the mind must be free of all disorder. If there is disorder in the functioning of the brain due to conflicts between the Old and the New Brain then what emerges from the Mind will get vitiated and so communication itself will be defective. The secret of communication lies not only in the technique of expression but in keeping the channels of communication free from all obstructions. J. Krishnamurti says in his book *The Urgency of Change:*

> When expression becomes all-important because it is pleasurable, satisfying or profitable, then there is a cleavage between expression and feeling. When feeling *is* the expression then the

conflict does not arise, and in this there is no contradiction and hence no conflict. But when profit and thought intervene, then the feeling is lost through greed. The passion of feeling is entirely different from the passion of expression, and most people are caught in the passion of expression.

If there is conflict between feeling and expression then that which is expressed will fail to touch the person to whom communication is directed. Both are necessary, Feeling and expression. We have seen in this chapter how one can refine and perfect the modes of expression. This is a process whereby channels of communication are being made more and more perfect. But what about the waters that flow through these channels ? The brain receives what the Mind sends, and through its perfected channels of communication helps it to move on to those for whom it is meant. But the Brain has no control over what is received from the Mind. And so while the technique of Expression is within the range of the brain, the Feeling is not. For this we must turn to the problems of the Mind in our inquiry into the deeper aspects of Meditation. Meditation demands not only the Birth of a revitalised Brain, it also requires the Death of the Old Mind and the Emergence of the THIRD WAY. Having dealt with the question of the birth of a revitalised brain, we must turn to the question of the death of the Old Mind and so come to the Emergence of a New Mind. When there is a clear line of communication between the New Mind and the Brain then there will be no conflict between Feeling and Expression. In this the Passion of Feeling and the Passion of Expression will exist together so that between experience and expression, between communion and communication there will be no gulf. When the brain supplies perfect channels of communication and the New Mind conveys pure and refreshing waters of life then will one experience the joys of Creative Living.

ELEVEN

THINKING WITHOUT THOUGHT

PATAÑJALI in the Third Section of his *Yoga Sūtras* says that *Dhāraṇā-Dhyāna-Samādhi* together form the spiritual discipline. He tells us that Awareness-Attention-Attunement cannot be separated one from the other. In fact, all the steps propounded by him in the *Yoga Sūtras* have to be practised simultaneously, and not successively. Yoga is a continuing process where from *Yama-Niyama* one moves on to *Samādhi*, and once again returns to the practices of *Yama-Niyama*. It is thus that one comes to a deepening of spiritual life. We have been discussing in these pages the triple-transformation, of the brain, the habit mechanism and the mind. This transformation process also has to be together, and not one after the other. The Brain, the Habit-mechanism and the Mind, they act and react upon each other. They cannot be divided into water-tight compartments. The increase of the brain-potential is as much a part of meditation as the discovery of the Third Way.

It is believed by many that first we must build the channels of Communication and then come to the experience of Communion; while there are others who talk of coming to the experience of Communion and then turn to the construction of communication-channels. Both approaches seem to lose sight of the wholeness of spiritual life. Here we find defects inherent in all exclusive approaches whether of Occultism or of Mysticism. In Occultism one is concerned with the construction of different channels of communication. But if there is no Communion, the channels must remain dry. Similarly in Mysticism one talks of Communion, the non-dual experience. But if there are no channels of communication available then the mystic experiences must get frittered away, as has happened, in ways that are abnormal. And so Communion and Communication must go together. It is said that the experience of communion will find its own ways of communication. It is true that the urge to communicate will arise as a result of mystic experiences, but if no instruments of communication are available then the urge will die away. Spiritual life demands a rhythm of Communion and Communication. Both these processes must go on simultaneously and not one after the other.

In the triple transformation about which we have been discussing, all the three factors have to be taken together, the re-vitalization of the Brain, the modification of the Habit-mechanism and the transformation of the Mind. If the brain is passive and working at a low-potential then the entire movement of meditation will get bogged. We started our discussion with the re-vitalization of the brain, because the brain is the nearest point for starting the spiritual journey. But this does not mean that one must first solve the problems of the brain and then go further. The increase of brain potential is a continuing phenomenon just as keeping the brain alert and active is a recurring process. The triple-transformation has to be together because the three factors involved in it cannot be separated. They are a living whole which cannot be broken up into fragments. For the purposes of our discussion we are taking them separately, for, thus alone the question can be understood intellectually in a clear manner.

We have already discussed in the earlier chapters the point that one of the functions of the Brain is to receive intimations from the Mind and to organise behaviour-patterns accordingly at the physical level. One may ask : What is the nature of the mind that sends messages and instructions to the brain out of which physical actions emerge ? Usually it is the mind steeped in its habit-mechanism that sends intimations to the brain. And so the behaviour-patterns and modes of action reflect the habit-oriented mind. It is the mechanical or the habitual mind that instructs the brain with regard to behaviour-patterns at the physical level. In other words in our actions there is reflected the urges of the mechanical or the habitual mind. Now the mechanical mind is past-oriented, but the human brain has to initiate actions that have relevance in the present. There is no wonder our behaviour-patterns are out of step with the requirements of the present. The sense reports coming to the brain are from the present, and the instructions coming from the habitual mind are of the past. And so normally we act in the present in terms of the past. Our response to the challenges of life which are always in the present are bound to be inadequate, for, how can the past meet the needs of the present ? J. Krishnamurti in his book *The Impossible Question* says :

> Thought is everlastingly conditioned, because it is the response of the past as memory. Thought is always mechanical; it falls easily into a pattern, into a groove although thought has certain limited freedom in its field, everything it does is mechanical, it is the outcome of the accumulated knowledge of the centuries. Thought is the response of the past.

Thus thought moves within the grooves of the past. These grooves are the habits of the mind. Faced with various situations of life at the physical level, we usually re-act, never or seldom act. Now a reaction is the outcome of habit. The habit-mechanism of the mind functions in terms of reactions. Our ideas, beliefs, even ideals, are, by and large, caught in the habit-mechanism. Similarly our actions at the physical level are very largely habit-oriented. And so both at the psychological as well as physical level we are stationed in the past, and from there organise our movements to meet the challenges of the present. When a response to a challenge is inadequate then a problem arises. There is no wonder our lives are beset with innumerable problems.

It would be interesting to find out as to how the mind passes on its habit-tendencies to the brain. It is true that the brain is the bridge between the body and the mind. But what is the form and nature of the load that has to pass over the bridge ? How are the habits of the mind passed on to the brain for being translated into bodily actions ? The brain sends sensations, processed into percepts, to the mind. These sensations are obviously from the present. But to the percepts transmitted to the mind, the mind sends back concepts that are based on memory to the brain. The brain's inquiry is based on the present, the mind's response is in terms of concepts arising from the past. The brain is activised by electrical impulses. But how does the Brain generate these electrical impulses without which it cannot organise actions and behaviour-patterns ? It has to be remembered that the mind speaks the language, not of words, but of images. And so it is through images that the mind transmits its instructions to the brain. Dr. Maxwell Maltz in his remarkable book *Psycho-cybernetics* says :

> Experimental and clinical psychologists have proved beyond a shadow of a doubt that human nervous system cannot tell the difference between an actual experience and an experience imagined vividly and in detail.

This means that when vivid images are transmitted by the mind to the brain, the latter is able to work on them as if they are actual happenings, and, not just imagined. These transmitted images act like fresh sensations so far as the brain is concerned. It is thus that the brain is able to induce the nervous system to initiate appropriate movements for the purposes of physical action. This is really the basis of all psycho-somatic illnesses. The root cause is the image transmitted by the mind. Unless this image is changed the illness, which is psycho-somatic, cannot be got rid of. The communication between the Mind and the Brain goes on in terms of images. If an image is not vivid then action initiated by the brain is insipid and colourless. It is the image that motivates behaviour-patterns through the brain. The mind does not know any other language save the language of images.

It is our common experience that in one's attempts to lead a religious or a spiritual life, one has to struggle against established behaviour-patterns. As we aspire to lead a spiritual life, we experience the greatest resistance offered by our modes of action and our behaviour patterns. We feel that some how we are unable to translate our ideals and beliefs into appropriate physical action. In the Mahābhārata, this difficulty has been expressed in the famous couplet which says that "even though I know what is good, I am unable to move in that direction, and even though I know what is evil, I am unable to refrain from it." This is the difficulty experienced by all spiritual aspirants. Our behaviour patterns are dependent upon the direction given by the mind to the brain. It is the function of the brain to implement what the Mind asks. The Brain fails to do this only if it is functioning at a low potential, or if the message transmitted by the mind lacks clarity. We have dealt with the question of brain-potential in the previous chapters of the book. We are now concerned with the messages sent by the mind to the brain for translation in terms of physical actions or behaviour-patterns. If the messages lack clarity, we must find out as to how this clarity can be imparted to the instructions sent by the mind. We are not concerned at this stage with the content of mind's messages. Our discussion at present has brought us to the point of clarity, for, if the messages are not clear then their translation into physical action will also show forth weakness and vagueness.

Ordinarily in our spiritual endeavour we say that it is because of the weak will that we are not able to translate our beliefs into appropriate behaviour-patterns. We believe that with the exercise of a strong will-power one would be able to bridge the gulf between belief and behaviour. And so in spiritual endeavour we grind our teeth and call out from within us strong will-power. But such exercise of will-power results only in struggle and resistance. The use of will-power for changing our modes of action brings into existence exhaustion and dissipation of energy. But if our modes of behaviour cannot be changed by the use of will-power then how is one to bring about this change? There is no doubt that our modes of action must be changed, for, they do not reflect what our ideals and aspirations indicate. The gulf between Belief and Behaviour is a begetter of tensions and frustrations in our life. We ascribe this to the existence of *tamas* or inertia in our nature, and we seek to break this inertia by the exercise of strong will-power.

One may ask: What is the role af Will-power if through its exercise one cannot change one's modes of behaviour? With the exercise of will-power we may suppress a particular behaviour-pattern, but this suppression itself becomes the cause of tension. Besides, the suppression of one type of behaviour is only a negative action. In spiritual life we want changes in our modes of behaviour of a positive nature. It is not enough that our behaviour shows absence of certain undersirable tendencies; it must contain good tendencies of a positive nature. What other instrument have we save the use of will-power for this purpose?

There is a great deal of misconception regarding that aspect of human consciousness which is described as Will, and, its functions. It is commonly believed that a person with a strong will-power has great capacity for resistance. In fact, the use of will-power is generally believed to be for the purposes of resistance. But this is completely erroneous, for, will is like a king who only gives orders. A king does not put his shoulder to the wheel in order to carry out the orders which he has given. It is left to his ministers to work out plans for the implementation of the orders and instructions given by the king. Thus, Will is the most quiet thing, needing no resistance. When it has given orders its function is over. With regard to the changes in behaviour-patterns and modes of action, it is not the function of Will to bring about necessary transformation. Its function is to give a direction as to what it wishes. To employ will in order to bring about actual changes is to lower the dignity of one who is a king in the realm of human consciousness. There is no wonder one is not able to change one's behaviour-patterns in a positive manner by the exercise of will-power.

The question is: What then is the instrument which carries

out the order of the king, and brings about actual transformation in our modes of behaviour? It is the image-building faculty of the mind. To build an image is to give form and shape to the directives given by Will. We are told that our thoughts have their forms. Sometimes the thought-forms are strong and vivid, but many a time they are weak and nebulous. It is the strong and vivid thought-forms that influence the person towards whom they are directed. It is these thought-forms which are the motivating force behind the sustenance or transformation of behaviour-patterns. These thought-forms are the images of the mind. We have stated earlier that the mind speaks the language of images or pictures. It knows no other language. Thus it is the image which is the speech of the mind, and it is through it that the directives of the mind are conveyed to the brain. The mind affects the body through the images that are transmitted to the brain. If we make a strong and vivid image of our friend on death-bed going through the last moments of the physical existence, then tears come to our eyes. The friend is not there physically, it is only his image. But the vivid image is as good as an actual happening to the brain and the nervous system and so the immediate effect is tears in our eyes. Or if we imagine a delicious meal in front of us our mouth begins to water even though it is not a physical meal, it is only a vivid mental image of the meal. This is the psycho-somatic phenomenon, where the image produces a change in physical response. It is the image that motivates our modes of behaviour. Once the matter is handed over to the image-building faculty of the mind, the power of will has no say. In giving orders and directives the will power has its full say. But once this is done the image-building faculty takes over and organises measures for their implementation. After this the will-power cannot intervene, or, if it does, it is powerless.

One can see the effect of images and the inability of will-power to intervene in our daily life. For example, we may feel nervous at public speaking, and an image of this nervous feeling has already been made. If after that we make a determined effort not to feel nervous when called upon to speak, we will find that in spite of our determination, when the actual moment of speaking comes, we do feel nervous. This is so because we have already made an image in which we visualise ourselves as feeling nervous, with our hands shaking as we hold the paper, reading our address. Once the image is made, a contrary use of will-power will have no effect. In fact, after the formation of the image, the king, that is, the will-power, has no right to intervene. A person may be called for an interview in connection with his job application. And he determines with a strong will-power that he will give all the answers with an air of confidence and that there will be no trace of nervousness at all. And yet when the applicant appears before his interviewers, he feels extremely nervous and is not able to give satisfactory answers to the questions put to him. This is so because an image was already made visualising oneself as feeling nervous. It is the image that acts, and not the will-power. As is our self-image so will be our actions at the physical level. The idea of transformation through image-building faculty has nothing to do with what is called 'positive thinking'. We shall presently see where the self-image psychology differs from positive thinking. In image-psychology the positive and the negative are combined. We shall find this out when we come to the mechanism of image-building with reference to one's behaviour-patterns.

Dr. Maxwell Maltz in his book *Psycho-cybernetics* has quoted a large number of cases which he treated in the course of his large practice as a Plastic surgeon. He has quoted an instance of a young man who went to the doctor saying he would like his slightly crooked nose to be corrected by plastic surgery. The doctor did the operation and the patient went away seemingly pleased with the surgical work done by the doctor. But after a few days the patient rushed back to the doctor saying his nose was as crooked as before and that the doctor had done nothing to correct it. The doctor showed him a mirror and asked him to see for himself whether the needed correction by plastic surgery had been done or not. But the patient would not accept even the verdict of the mirror. His self-image with a crooked nose had persisted and so he was unwilling to meet his friends or go to social functions. He felt that people would laugh at him seeing his ugly nose. He developed a strong inferiority complex just because the mental image of the nose remained. No power of will could work to change his behaviour born of a sense of inferiority. When the mental image was changed then his behaviour became natural, and, he was most happy to meet people, and that, too, without any feeling of inferiority. Such is indeed the power of image-building in the sphere of transforming one's behaviour patterns and modes of action.

The brain initiates behaviour patterns on the basis of the mage transmitted by the mind. It is not for the brain to question the rightness or otherwise of the image sent by the mind. It must carry out the intimations contained in the image. As is the image so will be the mode of physical action, and the more vivid an image, the quicker and sharper will be the pattern of behaviour. The Mind has a large number of well-established images, and the directive given by the Will is carried out in terms of these well-entrenched images. The image mechanism of the mind acts like the usual bureaucrat who never wants to deviate from his established ruts and red-tapism. He acts in terms of his habit and does not want to take the trouble to explore new ways of dealing with a problem. The habit mechanism of the mind functions by these well-established images. In fact due to this mechanism the directives of the will are distorted and sabotaged. The contact between the Mind and the Brain is done through images. And unless the habit-mechanism is radically modified, there is no chance of the directives of one's will getting a fair deal. The behaviour patterns will run along the habit-mechanism of images, and so the belief and behaviour will never come to a harmonious synchronisation. It is the image-mechanism that rules, and this mechanism is rooted in the habitual reactions and responses. There is no wonder our modes of physical action show no change in spite of our idealistic fervour, for, between the ideals and aspirations and the brain and the nervous system stands our habit-mechanism where well-entrenched images have been stored. We feel that our habitual behaviour is a die-hard, and, even though, we make tremendous efforts we are unable to make any appreciable change in it. Our habits and the well-established images are identical. And so if our habitual reactions and modes of behaviour have to be changed, it is the image-building process that will have to be tackled. No will-power to change patterns of behaviour will be of any avail. Our images, particularly our self-image, must undergo a radical change. We act as per the dictates of the self-image. All our actions and responses emanate from the self-image. It is this self-image which has built our second nature which we call as habit.

We are not going into the question as to whether the directives of the mind or the will are right or wrong. So long as the habit-mechanism, functioning through well-established self-image remains unchanged, so long there can be no possibility of changing our behaviour patterns. The increased brain-potential about which we discussed in the earlier chapters will make the habitual patterns of behaviour even stronger due to the greater energy with which it has been endowed in the wake of Kuṇḍalinī-arousal. The brain will do what the images indicate, and it will do this with great fervour when it possesses increased energy. And so the gulf between belief and behaviour will become all the more wide and unbridgeable.

We said that the psychology of self-image and positive thinking are not identical; in fact, they are completely different. In positive thinking there is an attempt to deal with behaviour-problem directly without changing the self-image. This is only another way of exercising will-power to change behaviour patterns. Any attempt along this line is bound to prove self-defeating, for, without changing the self-image to change the modes of action is to introduce an element of force or violence in this process. There must be a naturalness about one's behaviour. This cannot be when one employs the method of positive thinking. The problem of behaviour-pattern must be tackled through the image building-mechanism, and not directly as is sought to be done in exercise of will-power or in practices of positive thinking. When the self-image is changed then the behaviour patterns also will be naturally and effortlessly modified. No special effort needs to be made with regard to change in behaviour-patterns, for, they are dependent upon the images transmitted to the brain. With the modification of the habit-mechanism, and, therefore, with the modification of self-image, our problems of action and behaviour will pose no problem whatsoever.

The question is : How to change the self-image and thus bring about a radical modification in one's habit-mechanism ?

While quoting J. Krishnamurti we stated in the earlier part of this chapter that thought is habit-oriented and therefore functions from the past. In fact, thought is a slave to habit-mechanism. J. Krishnamurti in his book *The Impossible Question* says:

> Thought is the response of the past....Can the mind free itself from the habits it has cultivated....? Which means, can the mind be free from thought ?

If the mind is free from thought then what is the activity of the mind ? What is the functional content of the mind ? There is a vast difference between thinking and thought. Thought arises when thinking gets crystallised, or, one might say, thought is the dead-end of thinking. If there could be thinking without thought then would mind be free from habit enslavement. Thought is the crystallised image of thinking. Our usual movement of the mind is from thought to thought, that is from image to image. This movement is so rapid that we are never aware of the interval between the images. As thought process increases, the image gets stronger and stronger. Thus are the images strongly entrenched and become the motivating factor of habit-mechanism.

The Human Brain which initiates modes of physical action and behaviour does not come in touch with the living stream of thinking, its contact is only with thought or with the habit-mechanism. It is because of this that into the channels of communication, built by the brain, living waters of thinking never come. It is only the stagnant waters of habitual images that flow through them. As years roll by, the habit mechanism, with its images, becomes more and more rigid. The mind becomes so enslaved to this habit-mechanism that it loses its freedom. Our problem is : How to free the mind completely and totally ? and How to see that it does not get caught in the mechanical processes of habit-mechanism ? We will have to deal with the first question later when we come to the subject of the Transformation of the Mind. We are immediately concerned with the modification of habit-mechanism so that there may be established a direct contact between the Mind and the Brain.

But a question must arise: Since the mind knows only the language of images and pictures, how will there be a contact between the Mind and the Brain if the image-building mechanism ceases to exist ? And it is out of the images that habit gets formed. What will be the means of communication between the Mind and the Brain other than that of images? In the very act of thinking, forms and images come into existence, and without strong and vivid images the human brain cannot be induced to act. Thus images are necessary for new behaviour patterns and modes of action to come into existence. We seem to be on the horns of a dilemma. How is one to resolve it ? It is by exploring the subject of image building in depth that we can find a solution to this dilemma. Is it possible to have the image-building process to continue in its full intensity and yet not allow the images to get crystallised ? Can the whole habit-mechanism be evolved in such a manner that it functions in an extremely flexible manner, amenable to quick modifications ? Can the habit formation be so attenuated that it does not become a rigid structure ? Can images be held as long as necessary and then dissolved so as to make room for fresh images ? In other words can images come and go without bringing into existence rigid structures of habit-mechanism ? These are the problems which must be examined if newer and newer patterns of behaviour are to emerge. It is true that habit is the end-product of routine. But one cannot completely rule out the existence of routine in one's daily life. Without such routine there would be a great wastage of energy. The question is : Can one prevent the routine from becoming a rigid structure of habit ? If one could bring about modifications in one's routine from time to time, perhaps the rigidity of habit would not come into existence. But behind the maintenance of routine there exist images as the motivating factors. Routine needs the sustaining force of self-image. When the routine is broken the self-image gets disturbed. It is thus that a man becomes a slave to routine. If the self-image is changed from time to time then the enslavement to routine and habit will cease to exist. This will enable fresh images to come into being, and, it is these fresh images, clear and intense, that will induce the brain to establish new modes of action and behaviour. The interest of the brain gets diminished when it is required to establish behaviour-patterns on the basis of old and stagnant images. Our behaviour-patterns show forth repetitive tendencies because it is the old and deeply entrenched images that are transmitted to the brain from the habit-mechanism of the mind. In order to impart freshness to our behaviour-patterns it is necessary to have the transmission of fresh images. But this can happen only if there be clear and intense images which are kept free from getting caught in rigid habit-mechanism. One must learn the process of modifying habit mechanism from time to time if one is to be free from as terile and stagnant existence. A repetitive behaviour-pattern cannot have any livingness in it. And if one's modes of action are without such livingness, how can our communication with life around us be effective ? Spiritual life is a vibrant life, full of a quality of livingness which is easily displayed in all actions, howsoever small they may be. This is possible only when the images transmitted to the brain are fresh and alive. This is a very urgent problem of spiritual life, closely linked with the act of communication which we discussed in the last chapter. We must now examine the problem of image-building in depth to which we shall turn in the next chapter.

TWELVE

THE ROAD BIFURCATES

THERE are three major faculties of the Mind—they are the faculty of Reasoning, of Memory, and of Imagination. In reasoning one follows the laws and principles of logic. But these give to the process of reasoning a form and a structure. If one follows the laws of logic flawlessly then the structural form of reasoning will be sharp and orderly. By a logical process one can argue any case whether of the plaintiff or of the defendant. One can prove what one wants to prove by means of logic It is only a structural process. The content of reasoning is supplied, by and large, by memory and imagination. It is obvious that memory belongs to the past. Similarly imagination refers to the future. But so far as the activities of the mind are concerned, future is only a projection of the past, either negatively or positively. It is the unfulfilled past that needs future for its fulfilment. It is past as memory with its projection in future which is the content of imagination. Thus in one's imagination it is memory that occupies a place of prominence. Ernest Wood calls Imagination "the powerful spotlight of the human mind." This it certainly is because it is the most potent constructive force which the human mind possesses.

Imagination has various aspects. It appears as day-dreaming in the life of most people. It expresses itself as wishful thinking also. To many people, imagination is identical with fancy which has no basis in fact. There is scientific imagination, too, which builds up the whole by studying the part. This is what the science of paleontology does all the time. Whatever be the form of imagination, it is the past which gives it a content. It is possible to rid imagination free of all the memory content, but to this purity of imagination we shall come in the later chapters of this book. If imagination is the powerful spotlight of the mind then surely it must have both clarity and intensity. The spotlight must throw light in great intensity otherwise it is no better than an ordinary light. Moreover its beam of light must get focused on the spot that is sought to be illumined. Imagination can work as a dynamic constructive force only if it is intense and is capable of being focused.

In order to import these qualities of Clarity and Intensity to the act of imagination, it is necessary to understand the whole phenomenon of image-building, for, it is through image-building that imagination comes into existence. If the very process of image-building is defective then our imagination can never become the powerful spotlight of the mind which it is supposed to be. As is the image-building so will be the quality of imagination. We are not going into the question of purity of imagination where it is completely free from the content of the past. We take it that our imagination at present is rooted in the past. Even so it can exercise a powerful constructive force in the life of a man if there is both clarity and intensity in it.

We have stated earlier that by the very act of thinking, forms and images are created. When we say that our thinking is desultory or vague and weak, what is implied is that the images created by such thinking are out of shape. Sometimes we come across people whose thinking is so strong that one gets almost hypnotised in his presence. Strong thinking indicates the creation of clear and intense images. Our communication with each other is through images. Behind our words and gestures there are images, either strong or weak. Telepathic communication also depends upon strong and clear images. We send out thoughts to other people, whether helpful or otherwise, by the use of images. Thus the image-building mechanism contributes both to the change of one's behaviour patterns as well as to the helping of others by one's thoughts.

In any act of meditation, with or without method, the starting point has to be an image. It may be the image of a guru or a teacher, or it may be an image of a particular virtue-in-action, or it may be images called out by some mantra. We hear much about meditation being an act of observing one's thought-process. In any observation there must be something to observe. What is it that one observes in the observation of the thought-process ? Surely it must be the form of thought or the image created by the mind that one observes. One cannot observe the formless. For the observation of mind's images one does not need to have occult powers. When one visualises something, if it is clear and vivid, then the brain and the nervous system immediately become active. The brain perceives the image, regarding it as something that is actually happening at the physical level. The movement in the nervous system is proof of the visualisation of an intense image. In fact, when we make a vivid image we experience it as actually seeing it or feeling it. If the image is not vivid and strong then it serves hardly any purpose either for meditation or for sustaining or modifying the behaviour pattern. Thus a strong and vivid image is necessary for both the purposes. In the deeper movement of meditation, the image may and must drop away, but the beginning has to be with an image. By image we do not mean physical idols. Some people begin their meditation with idols, and others with mental images. There is hardly any qualitative difference between the two. How and when the images drop away in one's experience of meditation will be discussed in the later chapters. But before the image drops away there must be first the formation and the creation of an image. When we say that we are meditating on an idea, it is really the image formed by the mind. One must begin with the form before one moves on to the formless. Our first concern is with the form, its creation and its sustenance, before we proceed to the experience of the formless. In the strong and vivid visualization one sees the image which one can observe. The image may be visual or pertaining to any other sense, whether hearing or touch or smell or taste. To observe the strongly imagined object or happening does not require any super-physical power such as clairvoyance. In fact the strongly and vividly imagined experience can be so real that one can observe it as if it is actually happening at the physical level.

In our usual meditational practices we complain of our inability to concentrate or to hold any idea for any length of time. This means that our mental image slips away and we are not able to hold it. One can hold only a form, and the form of an idea is the image. We try to concentrate on the idea, and such concentration does not seem to succeed. It creates tensions and strains. Ernest Wood says that concentration should be attention without tension. Our efforts to hold an idea without enshrining it in a definite and vivid form are bound to be self-defeating. If only we would employ the image-building mechanism for the purposes of concentration we would easily be able to succeed and that too without creating any tension whatsoever. Concentration should be an act of attention, and this act becomes easy when the vague abstract idea is given a form and a shape in terms of an image. To start one's meditation without the creation of a clear and a vivid image is to be lost in vague and desultory thoughts. And our usual meditation is nothing beyond this, or it may be something like induced emotionalism. This is not meditation. Patañjali explains *Dhāraṇā* as Extensive Awareness, and meditation or *Dhyāna* as Totality of Attention. The secret of undisturbed attention lies in image-building. It is easier to observe an image than an abstract idea. And so the problem of image-building has to be considered both in depth as well as breadth. The path of image-building bifurcates as it proceeds. One way leads to the formation of behaviour-patterns and modes of actions through the stimulation of the brain. And the other way leads to the transformation of images into symbols where the deep experience of meditation is vouchsafed to the aspirant. It is here that the dropping of images takes place. We shall consider this aspect of our travel later. At present we are concerned with the first way where images help us to stimulate the brain towards establishment of modified patterns of behaviour.

This requires an understanding of the technique of Image-building. This technique is necessary for the initial stages of meditation as also for the transformation of our behaviour patterns. Upto the point of bifurcation, both the processes move along the same path. In fact there is only one path upto the point of bifurcation. The technique of image-building needs first an understanding of the question of creating clear and vivid images. We are unable to proceed in our medita ional practices because we have not turned to the creation of images. In fact, the image-technique has not been employed by us for our meditational purposes. Similarly for changing behaviour patterns also we have not employed the image-technique. We have believed that both the processes can be pursued by the exercise of will-power. To try to concentrate through will-power is to get tired and exhausted in the process. In the same way to attempt to change behaviour patterns through the exercise of will-power is utterly frustrating.

It has to be noted that the raw materials of all mental images come from our physical experiences. It is true that in these images certain modifications of physical happenings do take place — but, even then, the basic raw material comes from sensorial experiences. What we have seen or heard or otherwise sensorially experienced supplies the ground for the image structure of the mind. Since this is the case, the clarity of our mental images depends upon the clarity with which we have experienced physical events and happenings. If our sensorial experiences have been weak and vague then our mental images too are bound to be of the same nature. Sri Aurobindo says in his *Letters on Yoga* :

> An experience should be allowed its full time to develop or have its full effect. It should not be interrupted except in case of necessity .... During the experience the mind should be quiet. After the experience is over, it can be active. If it is active while it is there, the experience may stop altogether....

> To think and question about an experience when it is happening is the wrong thing to do; it stops it or diminishes it. Let the experience have its full play.... When it is over you can think about it, not while it is proceeding.

In order to have clarity and intensity in sensorial experience, it is of the fundamental importance that thought must not enter while the experience is proceeding. The sensorial experience must be allowed to have its full play without the interference of the mind. The entry of thought breaks up an experience and so both clarity and intensity are lost. We considered this matter in detail when we discussed the question of enjoyment without the enjoyer. The enjoyer obviously is the mind. If we can keep out the enjoyer then the experience will be able to have its full play. If the raw material for mental images comes from such total and complete sensorial experiences then the image-building technique will produce necessary results. The fullness of sensorial experience can be about anything — it may be the observing of a tree or a flower or a bird. If our observation of a physical object or event has been incomplete and defective then our mental image too will be blurred and indistinct.

Both for deeper meditational experiences and for the modification of behaviour patterns, the creation of a perfect image-building mechanism is essential. But can one consciously work at the perfection of this mechanism ? For the perfection of this mechanism there are two things which are necessary in the initial stage, that is upto the point where the bifurcation of the road comes as stated earlier in this chapter. These two things are the Creation of images, and the Holding of images. First of all, one must consciously work at creation of images. Such creation depends upon clear perceptions at the physical level. One can start with the simple geometrical designs. Just observe them clearly and closing the eyes make as faithful an image of the design as possible. From such designs one may move on to physical objects like chair, table, books etc. One can form the image of these objects with regard to shape as well as colour. It must be so clear and vivid that one almost sees them with closed eyes. This visual experience can be extended to other senses. From single objects one can move on to composite objects i.e. a number of objects in a room or in a lecture hall or anywhere. One can visualise clearly a room with all its furniture. One can experiment along this line taking rooms and houses at various places, near and far. One can vary this experiment in numerous ways, but the subject matter of such images must be some inert object or objects.

From this simple or composite inert objects, one can move on to living things, say a tree or a plant, or a flower, an animal or a bird. Make the image of a flower clear and vivid so that you see not only the shape and the colour of the flower, you also feel its texture, nay, you smell the fragrance of the flower as well. In image-building, one fact needs to be remembered, and that is, whatever is being imagined must be seen or experienced, not verbalised. To introduce verbalisation in image-building is to make the images diffused and vague. One must mentally see an object or feel it by touch or smell or taste. or hear its sound without mental verbalisation. It is only thus that the image becomes clear and intense. One may see a bird perched on the branch of a tree, with its beautiful colours and its magnificent plumage, say in the case of a peacock. One may see a cat, gracefully sitting, in a completely relaxed manner. Imagine these various living things in their context, see the light and shade of a natural scenery. The images must be so clear that one sees the nearby objects or living things, clearly and far away things in a diffused manner. In other words the mental images must be as far as possible such as to be completely faithful to what exists.

In one's experiments in image-building, one can move from static things and objects, to events, that have a factor of movement. One can imagine a flying bird, or a running cat or dog, or a moving vehicle. One can visualise a fast moving train or a faster moving aeroplane. Once again we have to note that the clearer the sensorial observation, the clearer will be the image of moving objects and things. Thus is image-building closely linked with the subjects we have discussed in the previous chapters with reference to increasing the absorbing power of the brain. We have, therefore, suggested that all subjects of triple transformation have to be considered together, for they form a whole with regard to the spiritual journey which takes us to the land of meditation.

In image-building just as one imagines a moving object or a bird or an animal or a train, similarly one can imagine oneself moving. Needless to say this movement itself is an image, and from there one observes whatever there is through the faculty of imagination. Or one can take a mental walk along some familiar road, and while thus walking, see, hear, smell, touch and taste in terms of clear mental images. There must not enter in this image-building process the element of mental verbalisation. When there is verbalisation, the image structure breaks down or it remains in the background, weak and hazy. By verbalisation one may call out images, but once the images have come in and are in process of formation, verbalisation must cease. In verbalisation, the mind describes what is to itself. In so doing the act of experiencing stops, or grows weaker and weaker.

We have talked of image-building more in terms of visualisation than in terms of other senses. But what applies to one sense-organ applies equally to other sense-organs. In fact, one should experiment on the above lines with all the senses, first separately, and then with all the senses together or with as many senses together as possible. One can visualise an orange with its shape and colour, the texture of its skin, the fragrance that it exhudes, the taste, sweet or sourish -- all these can be together so that it is a composite image. Our normal experiences with the outer world are of a composite nature, and so composite images would be nearer to actual experiences. In fact, such compositeness would give vividness and intensity to our images. In Image-building one can import a great deal of variety by experimentation along numerous lines. It would be a fascinating experiment which one can undertake at any time when nothing of a pressing nature compels our attention.

Image-building with regard to human faces and human situations is a little difficult, but if one has experimented along the above-mentioned lines then one can easily build images of human beings. Since our communications are mainly in the sphere of human relationships, the process of image-building with reference to human beings and human situations is absolutely necessary. One can begin by looking at a photograph or a picture of a friend or even of a stranger. If one can successfully create an image of the photograph or picture then one can move on to creating an image of the living human individual. From a single individual one can go on to a group of individuals and thence to human situations of a simple or a complex type. From a single inert object to complex human situation is a far cry, but one can cover this distance if one moves on systematically in the sphere of image-building.

Image-building is both an art as well as a science. One can help a person by thoughts, and that too very effectively. But for this a clear image of the person must be made. Having done this one can talk to this image in the same way as one would talk to a person actually and physically present. In cases of mental telepathy, too, creation of clear images is necessary as otherwise telepathic communication would not be effective. A clear image of the guru or the teacher, or a clear image with regard to the suject chosen for meditation helps one to keep mind's attention un-disturbed more easily than would be the case otherwise. It is true that in meditation all images must drop away — but they must first exist prior to their dissolution. And if the images prior to their being dropped are clear then their dissolution also becomes easier. We shall come to that aspect in the latter part of the book. We have stated that the path emanating from image-building bifurcates at a later stage. One path is image-building for communication, and the other path is image-building for communion. We are at present concerned with the image-building technique for communication.

In the image building process, it is not enough that a clear image has been formed or created. There has to be the holding of that image, and one must be able to hold the image as long as one likes. This is technically called *Dhāraṇā* which should be translated as Awareness instead of concentration. One can be really aware of an image only if one is able to hold it or keep it. The very meaning of the word *Dhāraṇā* is the act of holding. In our normal meditational practices this constitutes the most obstinate hurdle. We may be able to create a clear image, but by and large, we are unable to hold it. Why are we unable to hold an image? Why does it slip away from the hold of the mind? Is it possible for one to hold an image as long as one likes? It is only those images that we are able to hold that can be directed along whatever way one likes. But if the image slips out of the hold of the mind then surely such direction cannot be given.

We have considered in this chapter the validity and the importance of the technique of image-building both for communication and communion. In this connection we have discussed ways of creating different types of images. While the creation of images is one aspect of the instrument of communion and communication, the other aspect is the holding of the images so as to direct them along channels which one considers necessary. The subject of holding the images needs to be explored as exhaustively as possible. And so we shall turn to it in the next chapter. In the book entitled *Concentration and Meditation* published by the Buddhist Lodge, London, it is stated:

> The power of forming clear-cut mental images is essential to progress in meditation, and the more thoroughly it is developed the easier it will be to perform (those exercises that are needed for meditation).

We have seen how clear-cut images can be made, but the practical question is: How to hold them? The creation of clear-cut images would be meaningless if one is unable to hold them so as to direct them along the path of communion or of communication, or of both.

THIRTEEN

THE DETAILED BLUE-PRINT

IN THE entire universe, man is the only creature who is capable of conscious evolution. All other creatures depend upon Nature to initiate and guide their evolutionary process. Man has been able to free himself from the compulsions of Nature, even though as yet in a limited manner. This has been possible because man possesses the instrument of mind with all its various faculties. It is this mind which gives direction along which he intends his own evolution to move. Mind is the decision making entity which asserts, or tries to assert, its freedom against the determinism of Nature. But this mind is both the glory and the gloom of man. Its glory is evidenced in the achievements which man has been able to accomplish in various spheres of life, but more particularly in the field of science and technology. But the mind has also been the gloom of man inasmuch as it is unable to free itself from its own moorings in the past with the result that its decisions are far from right, not in the mechanical spheres, but in the psychological realm of man's life. Man has acquired his freedom but he is afraid of this very freedom. He wants freedom and security to move together. In reconciling the two irreconcilable factors, he has imprisoned his precious freedom within the confines of habit. Man feels that in the confines of habit alone he can be secure. It is thus that he allows his mind to move only in an area of limited freedom. The mind that is bound by habit is a mechanical mind. Man is still far away from knowing what a Creative Mind is. Now meditation is the experience of a Creative Mind, for, it enables man to free himself from the clutches of the Habitual Mind.

In order to tread this path leading to the experience of a Creative Mind, one must understand the habit-mechanism in which the activities of the mind are caught. A habitul mind is a repetitive mind, and all repetitive processes create dullness and passivity. What intimations of life's dynamism can such a mind pass on to the activised brain ? There is no wonder that our behaviour patterns and modes of action are habitual in nature. It is this habit which has made us mediocre. Our behaviour-patterns show no traces of our individuality. They are bound by habit and so are repetitive and monotonous. Habit may be described as tradition in man's psychological life. It is true that tradition has a place in man's life, for it is through tradition that there comes certain amount of steadiness in his life, both at the individual as well as the social level. But if this steadiness degenerates into dullness then such tradition is not a living but a dead tradition. Man has many such dead traditions in his psychological life. A living tradition is one which is able to absorb unto itself the eternal flux of life. Tradition and change constitute the rhythm of man's life. But man's habit-mechanism is allergic to change, for, it sees a danger to itself in such movement of life's flux. Thus does the mind of man alienate itself from the living stream of life. It begins to regard stagnant existence as identical with psychological security. How can such a mind impart any freshness to one's modes of action ? Our behaviour-patterns can almost be predicted, not only by ourselves but by others too. It is the unpredictability that gives charm to human relationship. The behaviour of a machine can be predicted, but not of a living entity. But if our behaviour-patterns come within the range of predictability then surely our life is no better than that of a machine. The habit-mechanism of the mind has brought us to stagnant and mechanical existence where joy and delight are for ever strangers. How to combine tradition and change in our psychological life ? A dead tradition and change can ill go together; it is only the living tradition that can co-exist with change. To sift the living from the dead, and to prevent the living tradition from becoming dead — this indeed is what is meant by modification in one's habit-mechanism. We are at present not concerned about the nature of change. To this we shall turn when we discuss the subject of the transformation of the Mind. Our concern just now is to see that the traditions of our psychological life remain for ever alive and not become dead. It is only a living tradition that can contain changes that come from sources near and far. Thus alone can a freshness be imparted to our behaviour-patterns and our modes of action. When the brain receives mind's impulses emanating from the centres of living traditions, and not from the dead ones, then our physical actions too can show forth a dynamism of a throbbing life, and not the dullness of dead traditions and mechanical habits. A framework of Living Traditions serves as a vessel to receive the New Impulses that come from the transformed and the transforming mind. To create such a framework demands constant modifications in one's habit-mechanism. H.P. Blavatsky says in her *Voice of the Silence*:

> Mind is like a mirror, it gathers
> dust while it reflects.

It is this gathering of dust that imparts rigidity to mind's habit-mechanism. One has to blow off this dust constantly. It is this which we have termed as the modification of Habit-mechanism. This has to be done constantly lest there be the gathering of the dust, making the mirror dull in its reflecting capacity.

The question is : How to change one's habits so that the vessel of Living Traditions remains clean and bright, ready to receive the New Impulses of life ? When the habits of the mind change then there comes about naturally a change in the patterns of one's behaviour at the physical level. In the change of habits one normally employs one's will-power, but this produces resistance and consequent exhaustion without effecting any change in one's patterns of habit. We saw in the last chapter that the function of Will is to give orders and instructions. It is the decision-making faculty of the mind. It gives a direction as to what must be done, but it has nothing to do with bringing about actual changes. It is not within its power to bring about modification in habits nor in modes of physical action.

This task is done by Imagination through its image-building faculty. Will must not enter the field which belongs to Image-building. If it does, it is bound to feel humiliated. Dr. J.J. Van Der Leeuw says in his book *Gods in Exile:*

> When M. Coure, in his epoch-making exposition of the power of imagination, or the creative power of thought, said that when the will and the imagination are at war the imagination always wins, he was quite right.

It is undignified for will to enter into a fight with imagination or the image-building faculty. When the image is formed embodying the decision of the will then it is the Image that is in full command of the situation. The changes to be brought about in habit-mechanism and through it, in behaviour-patterns can be done only by the image-building faculty and never by the exercise of Will-power, howsoever strong it may be. The following words of Dr. J. J. Van Der Leeuw will help us to understand the problem of Imagina ion and Will a little more clearly :

> Consider the example of a man craving for drink. He knows the misery caused by his weakness, he knows how it wastes his wages and starves his family and, in his sane moments, he determines to give it up. Now he passes a place in the street where he can get drink, sees people go in and out, and perhaps even smells the drink. Upto that moment he is safe from temptation, safe from struggle; but what happens now ? In that short fraction of a second, he imagines himself drinking; he makes a thought-image and for a moment lives and acts in that

thought-image of himself enjoying his drink. He feels how it satisfies his craving, but in reality it has only increased it and made the ensuing action almost unavoidable. Then having created the image, he belatedly calls upon his Will and says : "I do not want to do this thing". But then it is too late, then the struggle is practically futile. Once the thought-image has been created, realization in action generally follows.

If the thought-image is weak one can suppress a particular action, but then this suppression brings into being struggle and consequent exhaustion. The best way is to prevent the thought-image from being formed, for, then the particular action will not materialise. A strong image gets immediately transmitted to the brain. When it reaches the brain then one comes to a point of no return. The brain starts working on the image without any delay since it is the instruction coming from the mind. And the processing of the image by the brain results invariably in that mode of action which is indicated by the Image. With no power of will can the image be called back once it has reached the precincts of the brain. Dr. J.J. Van Der Leeuw discusses this in his book by giving an illustration from our common life in the following words :

> When we learn to ride a bicycle and, seeing a solitary tree in our way make straight for the one obstacle which is sure to bring us to grief, our mistake lies in an uncontrolled imagination; we allow ourselves to imagine that we are going to hit the tree, create a thought-image of ourselves doing that and then strengthen it by emotion in this case, fear. Then we begin to resist it...

Here the author speaks of the damage being caused by the uncontrolled imagination. What does this mean ? Can imagination be controlled ? If so, by whom and how ? Surely it is not the power of will that can control imagination. Once the image has been built, it cannot be controlled by will. Can imagination be controlled before the image-building has taken place ?

In order to understand this question of the controlled and uncontrolled imagination, one must examine as to how ordinarily our image-building mechanism functions. With most of us the image-building process is motivated by external events, objects or happenings. We see something, or hear something and immediately an image is formed. And by a process of association the image becomes strengthened. The stimulation for the image obviously comes out of memory with which objects or events have associations. The memory stimulates various images, and by further association they get greatly intensified. But memory and its associations are a part of the habit-mechanism, and so the images that are stimulated by memory on experiencing something from outside are habitual images. They remain stored in habit-mechanism and are sustained by mental habits. It is these that are the uncontrolled images. They have not been formed by conscious working of the mind. These images are unconscious or habitual. And since the conscious mind has no control over them, these images carry away the mind with them. It is to this that the Bhagavad Gītā refers in the following verse appearing in its Second Discourse :

> O son of Kunti, the excited senses of even a wise man ... impetuously carry away his mind.

The uncontrolled images emanating from the habit-mechanism of the mind reach the brain and through it the senses. When the senses get excited due to the impact of the habitual images there is the emergence of physical actions giving expression to the urges of those images. In habit-mechanism the images get more and more intensified due to constant repetition. Whenever one sees something or hears something or experiences something with other senses, the brain sends a message to the mind. This message is snatched by memory with the result that the habitual images are released in response to brain's intimation. It is a vicious circle between the senses and the brain on the one hand, and the memory and habit mechanism on the other. Over this unconscious or habitual images ordinarily the mind has no control. When the psychological memory is aroused due to such intimations of the brain about which we have spoken, then it acts so powerfully that the conscious mind is almost kept in the background. It is the mind thus rendered passive which is carried away by the onslaught of the senses. It is quite obvious that this uncontrolled image-building process must be brought under control as otherwise one will remain a slave to them, feeling helpless under its impact.

But the uncontrolled image-building process cannot be brought under control by will power. The control can be brought about only by a conscious process of image making. Our images are ordinarily stimulated from outside. The initiative of image-building is not with us but with outer events and objects. In controlled image-building, however, the initiative comes from within and not from without. If one learns the technique of conscious image-building then the uncontrolled images will cease to have their sway. We discussed in the last chapter various methods by which conscious image-building can be undertaken with great success.

But will these conscious thought-images break the spell of unconscious images which have gained momentum in the course of repetitions over a number of years ? A mere thought-image even if consciously built, is much too weak to stand against the well established habitual images. A thought-image has to be surcharged with emotion, for, then only it gets vitality. A thought-image may have clarity, but it is emotion that gives it intensity. In a consciously created image there must be the full involvement both of thought as well as emotion. The fresh image with great vitality imparted to it by emotion has tremendous power against which the habitual image cannot cross swords. The habitual images have their momentum due to constant repetition, but a fresh image has a vitality of a living entity, not of something that is old and has to be awakened by constant floggings from outside. But the fresh image must have fullest involvement in it both of thought as well as emotion

We said in the last chapter that our problem is to hold an image which has been consciously created. The image seems to slip out of our hands constantly, and so we are never able to hold it. And unless we hold it, we cannot direct its course. We are not able to hold our images because they are merely thought-images with no emotional content in them. A mere thought-image which is inherently weak cannot withstand the strength of the habitual images which have developed their own vested interests. They go on with an urge to continuity, and in the mere thought-image there is no such urge. And so unless a thought-image is fully charged with emotion there is no chance of man getting out of the compulsions of the uncontrolled images.

It is this lack of emotional content in our mental images that is the cause of distractions in the usual meditation practices. Our mental images with which we start our meditation have no emotional content, or very little. But an emotional content can come only if one is intrinsically interested in the subject chosen for meditation. If the subject itself does not interest us then how can one bring an emotional content into it ? and so the consciously built images must be such in which we are primarily interested. It will be easy to make such images and also put into them emotional intensity. We can hold images easily when they are clear and at the same time intense. In other words, there will be no difficulty in holding images if there is the full involvement of thought and emotion. We saw the technique of making conscious images, from the object that is inert to the highly complex human situations. By and large, the emotional content will come from human situations. But the conscious image of this nature will be possible only if we have experimented with the earlier stages of image-building. The initiative for such image-building must not rest with outer objects or events. The initiative must be with ourselves so that the images are created from within and not motivated from without. These consciously created images with powerful emotional content in them will cause a breaking up of the citadel of habitual images, namely the habit mechanism itself. It may not break up at the first instance, but it is sure to get disintegrated when consciously created images, with powerful emotional content, start their own functioning. We have seen that there are two conditions which need to be fulfilled for the holding of images. One, they must be emotionally charged, and two, they must arise from within and not from without. One can choose one's own subject of intrinsic interest engage oneself in the task of image-building.

One may say that supposing the subject of interest is mundane, how can one begin one's meditation with such mundane things ? For meditation, subject is of no importance whatsoever, because whatever subject one chooses for meditation, it has to be dropped, because in the inner precincts of meditation no subject is permitted to enter. All subjects, even the noblest, must be left behind, for, before one enters the inner sanctuary of meditation one has to be divested of everything, of all metals and valuables, not so much in the physical sense as in the psychological sense.

One may ask : What will be the freshly created images containing an emotional intensity, do ? How will our behaviour patterns be changed ? How will such images rid us of the habitual modes of action ? Our problem is not just to create and hold mental images. Our concern is to see how they can become effective where the exercise of will power seems to fail ? To hold images of subjects in which we are primarily interested would be a matter of pleasure, and not of pain. Such images will be charged with emotions that are pleasurable, and pleasure itself will be conducive for releasing mental energy. And so these consciously created images will have their dynamism such as habitual images can never have. Needless to say these tremendously surcharged images will touch the brain with a great impact. When this happens the brain alerts the nervous system so that both of them begin to treat the impact as an actual physical happening. The impact of the habitual image can never be so powerful as these consciously created fresh images with an emotional content of great energy.

There is one factor which needs to be noted, and that is that these consciously created images must reach the brain without the frittering away of its energy. The process of energy-dissipation must not start as otherwise the images will lose their vitality.

This is possible only when the mind holds the image but does not indulge in it. With indulgence the energy will soon get dissipated with the result that its impact on the brain will be very feeble. In indulgence it is not the mind that holds the image; it is the image that holds the mind. In such a condition the mind cannot direct the flow of image-energy. The mind must hold the image in such a manner that it can leave off its hold over it in no time. One can hold the image of this nature for any length of time without any difficulty due to the pleasure-principle involved. And yet the pleasure-principle must not move in the direction of indulgence. This is what *Vijñāna Bhairava* speaks about in the following sūtra which we quoted earlier also.

> Keep attentive on the fire in the beginning, and so continuing, avoid the embers in the end.

These mental images with thought-emotion involvement must be strong, vivid and three dimensional with as many details as can be projected into them. The images should not be flat like pictures, but as true to living things and beings as possible. When one holds the image one must get a feeling that one is holding something that is actually present in front of us.

But what is one to do by holding these images ? They must be passed on to the brain for necessary action and implementation. It is not the brain that must snatch away the image, but the mind must hand over the image to it. The more vivid and detailed the image is, the more perfect is the translation of it in modes of action and patterns of behaviour. The holding of the image is the point from where the path bifurcates as we stated in the last chapter. From here one stream goes towards communion and the other towards communication. We are at present concerned with communication and so must see the path as it turns towards it. How does the holding of the image and then passing it on to the brain help us in dealing with problems of communication ?

In our discussion we are mainly concerned with the change in our behaviour patterns, moving away from habitual modes of action to new and fresh patterns of behaviour. And so the image that is consciously created and held without indulgence would be of new patterns of behaviour that we wish to become actual at the physical level. If one's present behaviour displays nervousness when called upon to do certain things, then let there be a clear, vivid and three dimensional image where one sees oneself acting without the slightest trace of nervousness. Let this image be as clear and vivid as possible. One of the important points to be borne in mind is that the image must be of the desired thing happening in the present, and not wishing that it may so happen in the future. One must see oneself in that image as behaving in a new manner in a variety of circumstances. If one brings in the element of future then it implies a use of will power for effecting the desired changes. The brain has to be impressed that certain things are happening at present, for, then alone, it, along with the nervous system, sees them as an actual event. The imagined becomes actual only when the present tense is introduced in the image-building.

One may make a vivid and a three dimensional image of anything that one desires to be translated into physical modes of action. Play about with that image so that there is no tension in the holding of the image. The holding must be in a state of relaxation and yet with intensity. It is in such a state of the mind that the image can be handed over to the brain. This handing over is not a special ceremony. When the hold of the mind over the image is released then the brain takes it over — in fact, the brain is too willing to take it over because of the clarity and the intensity which have been imparted to those images. For the brain it is identical with the actual physical happening and so becomes activised to process it in appropriate physical action.

One may ask: How does the brain do it ? Some of us have employed image technique sometimes. But most often we introduce in this technique the element of future. And so with the image there comes a resolve saying to ourselves that in future we will act in the manner indicated by the image. But the brain acts in terms of the present and never in the context of the future. Not only has the image to be in the context of the present, it has also to be a positive image and not a negative one. If one is concerned with changing one's behaviour-pattern it is necessary that one makes a positive image in which one sees oneself as behaving in that manner. The image must not only be vivid, it must contain as many small details as possible, and above all it must be a living image, in terms not of the future but of the present. This positive image must contain a feeling of pleasure and not a feeling of compulsion. One must see oneself in that image as enjoying the new mode of behaviour. It is this factor of enjoyment that will give added vitality to the image. Under the impact of the image the brain will feel motivated by pleasure and not by pain or compulsion. We have seen in earlier chapters that this feeling of pleasure gives to the brain an increase of energy. One may still ask : How does the brain bring about a change of behaviour as desired. We must understand the role of three instruments of our consciousness. The Will is the giver of direction; it indicates what must be the new pattern of behaviour. On the basis of this directive, the image-building faculty prepares a detailed blue-print. In the present case it is a three dimensional blue-print, one might say it is a model based on the directive of the Will. Then this model or blue print is handed over to the engineer which the brain is. The brain puts up a construction along the lines of the blue-print or the model. These three faculties must confine their activities to their own respective spheres, and not encroach upon the sphere of others. If this is done then the whole process moves on efficiently and smoothly.

The brain is like a computer, far more complex than any computer invented by modern technological science. And like any other computer it can function efficiently only when it is fed properly. If it is not fed aright then it cannot give right solution to any problem placed before it. The feeding of the brain is done at two ends. One is the sensorial end, and the other, is the mind-end. We have discussed, how, when sensorial experiences are not interrupted by the entry of thought, the brain gets clear and undistorted reports from the various senses. This is the right feeding of the brain through the sensorial channel. But there takes place the feeding of the computer which the brain is from the mind This is done through images. If the mental images are clear, vivid and intensely living then the brain gets activised almost as effectively, if not more, as it would be under sensorial impacts. The computer is expected to solve problems presented to it. It has to be fed with problems which are rightly and clearly formulated. It is the function of Will to formulate the problem, the direction along which it wants new behaviour-patterns to come into being. The clear directive given by the power of will is the formulation of the problem. It is the image-building faculty that gives shape and form to this problem in terms of clearly built images. When these images are surcharged with emotion then they are ready to be handed over to the computer-agency of the brain. And like a good computer, the brain evolves a solution in terms of new behaviour patterns.

Many of us have unconsciously experimented with the question of new habit-formations. For example, if one is habituated to rise late in the morning, and wants to develop a new habit of early rising, one strongly resolves, before retiring to bed, that one is determined to rise early next morning, come what may. The result of this determined resolve is that we get up early but without having any restful sleep. We get up several times during the night to look at watch lest we oversleep. This constant looking at the watch must give us disturbed sleep. We are unable to go on with this resolve for any length of time, and so we give up the effort, or if it continues we remain in a perpetual state of tension due to insufficient sleep. Instead of using the will power, one should create a strong and a vivid image where one sees oneself rising early and enjoying it. In this image one listens to the chirping of the birds in the early morning, and one is able to inhale the fresh morning air. If such an image, vivid and clear, is made, with whatever details one can put into it, then in a few days one will be able to rise early, naturally and effortlessly. The image creates a new mode of action wiping away the traces of the old habit. It needs to be remembered that the imagined, happening must be in the present, and one must see oneself enjoying the new mode of behaviour. The image to be passed on to the brain must contain this factor of pleasure or enjoyment.

Just as the brain wakes us up without our being subjected to sleepless nights as described in the above instance, one can experiment with various habits to which one is addicted and from which one is struggling to be free. Such a habit may be of smoking or of drinking or any other. One will find that by the technique of image-building one can get rid of the old habit in no time and that too without a struggle. If it is the habit of smoking then one can make a strong image of the new behaviour and see oneself enjoying the new way of living. One may imagine oneself in the midst of smokers, and yet one finds oneself enjoying the new role, feeling no inducement to smoke again. We have stated that the image must be a positive one, not one in which we find ourselves engaged in fighting the old habit. The more one resists the old habit, the stronger it becomes. It must be left alone to wither away, and it will wither away when no nourishment is given to it. With a positive, exuberent and vivid image one must move on activising the brain along new lines of behaviour-patterns.

But one must not forget that the new modes of behaviour also can become centres of new habit-mechanism. If this happens then we will be caught in another monotonous, stale and mechanical living. With regard to habits there is no question of good or bad. There may be new habits and old habits, but there is nothing good or bad about them. Every habit causes constriction to one's fresh and natural living. And so the new habits too must go the same way as the old habits. J. Krishnamurti says in his *Commentaries on Living* (Third Series) :

> The cultivation of habit, however good and respectable, only makes the mind dull.

And so the new modes of action initiated by the vivid and clear images may also become new habits, and thus in place of the old habit mechanism one may bring into existence a new such mechanism. If this happens then the mind will degenerate itself into dullness and passivity once again. To have the image-building mechanism functioning most efficiently, and yet not to allow it to bring into existence a habit-mechanism — it is this which is most imperative if man is not to shift from one slum area of the mind to the other.

How is one to prevent this from happening ? Can there be routine without that routine becoming a habit ? Routine there must and will be in life, for, it saves the wastage of time and energy. A routine is a particular mode of behaviour. But a mode of action has its structure as well as its spirit, it has a form of conduct as well as a life giving content. The form and the structure need to be changed from time to time, as otherwise they tend to become rigid and unresponsive. To establish new routines and fresh modes of action is necessary for healthy living. It is thus that the habit-mechanism gets loosened, It is possible to break up the rigidities of one's habit-mechanism by conscious image-building.

But every action has its structure and its spirit. It is good to keep the modes of action fluid and flexible so that they may be able to express even subtle nuances sent by the mind. But if the new forms and structures are not imbued with new spirit then we shall be witnessing a phenomenon of Old Wine in New Bottles. It is necessary to have New Bottles but it is also imperative that New Wine must be poured into them. But from where will this New Wine come ? The Mind functions from its background of likes and dislikes and therefore what it pours is coloured by these tendencies. It is capable of initiating new forms, but is unable to inspire a new spirit. It moves along the path of modifications but it never knows what a mutation is. It functions on the plane of continuity, and from there it can move into modified continuity. But it never knows what the experience of Discontinuity is. And yet the new wine comes only in moments of discontinuity. Mind caught in rigid habit mechanism gets imprisoned in the prison house of continuity. Through conscious image-building, mind can begin to function in the new realm of Modified continuity. And it is this that we have discussed in these pages. Through modified continuity new forms and structures of behaviour can come into existence. And this is necessary because thus alone flexible and fluid forms and organisations can come into being. These fluid forms will be able to receive the New Impulses when they arrive. If there are rigid forms present then the New Impulse will have no place to enter. One does not know as to what will be the nature of the New Impulse. But if one keeps forms and structures in a flexible and fluid condition then whatever be the nature of the New Impulse it will be able to use them and mould them to suit its purposes. If our modes of action and behaviour have become rigid and unresponsive then they will be of no use to the New Impulse. This is so both at the individual as well as the collective level. If by constant and conscious image-building one initiates modifications in forms and structures so that no particular form becomes rigid, then these forms will become suitable vessels in which to receive the New Wine.

We have come to the point of bifurcation in our spiritual journey. With the creation and the holding of the consciously formed images, we come to a point where one road leads us to the fields and plains of communication, while the other takes us to the summits of communion. Upto the point of holding the thought-emotion image, the road is common. From here the consciously created images are handed over to the brain for initiating new patterns of behaviour and action based on those images. The images are put in charge of the brain-computer directing it to find solutions to the problems of action and behaviour approrpriate to the needs of the situation. Once the images are handed over one must not interfere with the working of the computer. One must forget all about it, for, if one interferes with the functioning of the computer, that is the brain, then there will be confusion and chaos. When one plants a seed in the soil, one does not disturb the soil again and again to find out whether the seed has sprouted or not. The seed is being looked after by the soil. Similarly once the problem, in the form of a newly constructed image, has been handed over to the Brain it must be left to the brain to find out as to when and how the solution will be given. There is no doubt that the solution will come. And when the brain is greatly energised due to the flow of Kuṇḍalinī energy it is bound to give us an answer as speedily as possible. But the brain must be left free to work out the solution. The brain will evolve necessary channels of communication, that is, the patterns of behaviour needed in the context of the problem posed by the image. From the holding of the emotionally charged images this road to communication begins. But from this very point another road leads to the mountain top of communion.

Even though image-building mechanism functions at the conscious level, the quality of mind remains unchanged. And so, the consciously built images carry only the dictates of the old mind. The decisions and directions on which the image-building mechanism works are those of the old mind. Such decisions are conditioned by the background of the mind, its likes and dislikes. And so while the forms and structures of behaviour do undergo a change, the spirit inspiring them is one that emanates from the old mind. A mere structural change will not do, there has to be fundamental change in the spirit that must inspire the New forms.

But for this we must move along the mountain path which leads to communion. It is in the moments of communion that a fundamental transformation of mind takes place. When this happens then the Mind is imbued with a new quality. When the New Quality inspires the New Forms then there is New Wine in the New Bottles. From the New Quality of the Mind will emerge new dynamic images which will bring an entirely new spirit to the modes and patterns of man's behaviour at the physical level.

One may ask : Does one carry with oneself the images that one has created and has held with emotional fervour on this mountain path of communion or does one leave them behind ? If they have to be left behind then why should one hold them ? On the mountain path one does carry the images but with a different purpose. Along the path of communication the images are transmitted to the brain, in fact the brain is filled with them. But along the path of communion the images are emptied of their content. The first is a filling process, the other is an emptying process. Both are needed for the wholeness of the spiritual path. But after the experience of communion, are images needed at all ? If not, what is the purpose of building up the image-mechanism with such toil and labour ? Even after the experience of communion, images are necessary, for, the means of communication is only through images. After Communion there have to be images, as it were, from moment to moment. Such images have a momentary existence, for, every moment, that is, every psychological moment, sees the emergence of new images. Such is the dynamism generated by the experience of communion that its communication demands a New Image. For this the image-mechanism has to be extraordinarily alert, so that it creates new images under the impact of new impulses arriving from the experience of communion. The old images can serve no purpose in this act of communication.

If this be so then the old mind must die for the New Mind to come into being. This is so, for, the experience of meditation demands the death of the old mind. But if the old mind dies, what about the experiences and talents that it has gathered ? Are they of no use ? J. Krishnamurti in his book *The Flight of the Eagle* says:

> The eagle in its flight does not leave a mark, the scientist does. Inquiring into this question of freedom, there must be not only scientific observation, but also the flight of the eagle that does not leave a mark.

The death of the old mind does not mean the wiping away of all the technique that it has learnt. It means divesting the old mind of all its content. The technique of the old mind with the content of the new mind — this is indicated in the above passage of J. Krishnamurti. And so the technique of image-building must remain in all its perfection, but the content must be totally emptied. When this happens then the image-building mechanism is imbued with new content from moment to moment.

This new impulse is not the product of the old mind, it arrives in the moment of its death. It is the content of the New mind that is poured into the vessels created by the technique of image-building. When the brain receives the vivid and clear images transmitted to it, it works at new patterns of behaviour so as to enable these structures to be imbued with the Fresh Spirit of Communion. Then the modes of action are not only new in form but are new in spirit too. There is a new quality in behaviour patterns at the physical level. The ever fresh images by their functioning prevent a rigid habit-mechanism from coming into existence. Every image is new and so every mode of action is new. The harvest of the old mind is its technique. This is not rejected, but into the technique of the old mind is poured the scintillating message of the new.

How to combine the flight of the eagle with the technique of the scientist ? How to move along the mountain path of communion, taking the consciously created images with all their emotional content, and yet get them emptied ? What happens when the images are emptied ? What then will be the meeting point between Communion and Communication ? These are the questions that bring us to the threshold of the Transformation of the Mind, the core and the crux, the secret and the mystery of Meditation.

FOURTEEN

THE OVER-FLOW OF NATURE

THERE is a fundamental principle of education which says that in any educative process one must move from the known to the un-known, from the near to the far. It is this principle which we have adopted in our discussion of the subject of meditation in these pages. We have moved from the near to the far. For us the body and the brain are the nearest. For our healthy bodily living, the brain has to be very efficient. Besides, in this age of fast movement in all spheres of life, the question of adjustment and adaptation has assumed a place of great importance. And for us at the physical level, brain is the only instrument of adjustment. It is because of this that we started our discussion with the brain, its relaxation, its potential of work, its orderliness and also its channels of communication. It was in this context that we examined the question of awakening Kuṇḍalinī in a spontaneous way, utilising for this purpose the functioning of the pleasure-principle. We saw that the brain potential can be increased enormously by the spontaneous awakening of Kuṇḍalinī.

The discussion of the problem of communication with reference to the brain brought us to the threshold of the mind. The brain is required to channelise the intimations of the mind so as to trasmit them in an effective manner in terms of appropriate behaviour patterns and modes of action. We saw that the mind communicates with the brain in the language of images, and so in the modification of behaviour patterns it is the image-building faculty of the mind that has to function with great efficiency. When the consciously built images are strong, vivid and intensely alive then the brain and the nervous system take them for actual happening. The brain immediately works on them so as to translate them in suitable modes of action. We saw that it is not by the exercise of will-power but by transmission of vivid images that one can bring about modifications in behaviour-patterns.

It needs to be mentioned that we are not suggesting that by image-transmission we can build virtue after virtue in our character. The images built by the mind have the same content which the mind has gathered in the course of time. If there are anger or greed or ambition in the make up of the mind, whatever images it builds are bound to contain these tendencies. By mere image building and transmitting them to the brain one cannot free the mind of these traits. By image-building hate cannot be transmuted into love. What the image-building can do is to alter the expressional patterns of these tendencies. One may be extremely arrogant by nature, and may be used to express this arrogance in an extremely nasty manner by being rude and abrupt. This may create difficulties for oneself, and great deal of annoyance to others. One cannot change this expressional trait by the use of will. But one can change this trait by strong and vivid-image-building and transmitting those images to the brain. One does not get rid of one's arrogance but one can express it in a less nasty and abrupt manner, showing forth something of mellowness and softness in one's behaviour. Hate cannot be changed into love either by will-power or by image-building. But by image-building the expressional modes of hate can be changed so that one is not cruel but considerate towards the feelings of others. And so by image-building it is the behaviour pattern that is sought to be changed. The content is the same, coming from the conditioned mind, but the way of expressing this content can be altered so that one does not provoke others by one's behaviour. Besides this, one can bring about modifications in one's habits to a large extent by the technique of image-building. This is a path of modification, not of fundamental transformation. And most people would like to turn to modifications before they undertake the arduous journey towards fundamental transformation. Moreover this technique of image-building enables us to create fluid and flexible modes of action which can become suitable vessels for the receiving of New Impulses as and when they come. The technique of image-building enables one to present one's ideas in new forms and patterns. The content is the same but the presentation is different. One can understand the possibilities as well as the limitations of this technique of image-building by the following words of the great mystic poet, Rabindra Nath Tagore, who addressing his disciple in one of his poems, says:

> Disciple, you were asked to tune the instrument,
> who asked you to sing ?
>
> You were asked to carve a throne with all your skill,
> but who asked you to occupy the throne ?

The mind, through the image-building technique, can tune the instrument, but it cannot sing. The song of the mind will be no better than cacophony, for, it cannot but be full of discord and disharmony. The conditioned mind, with all its conflicts, can sing a song that can never be pleasing to the ears. But the image-building faculty can do the tuning of the instrument, or it can, with skill and ingenuity, carve a beautiful throne. But if it occupies that very throne then there will be chaos and anarchy in the kingdom over which it rules. To keep the tuned instrument untouched and to keep the skilfully carved throne unoccupied, it is this which speaks to us of what the image-building technique can do, and what it cannot and must not do. The mind, through this technique, can forge beautiful forms, but it must not put its ugly content into them. The new forms and modes of behaviour must be kept ready to receive the content that may come from beyond the mind. The doors of the house must be kept open lest the Divine Guest turn away, finding the doors and windows closed. It is the new behaviour-patterns, ever fresh, due to the consciously created images and imbued with vitality, that will serve as open doors, for, they will be flexible and fluid, ready to receive the Divine Visitor from wherever He mäy choose to come. We have dealt with the question of new behaviour-patterns coming into existence due to the impact of fresh images, strong and vital, on the brain greatly energised with the force of Kuṇḍalinī released in a spontaneous way. But the question is : What about the new content, the New Wine for the New Bottles ?

The New Content cannot be given by the old mind conditioned as it is by the background of a thousand yesterdays. The old content must go before the new can arrive. The mind must be emptied of its content even though it preserves its skill and technique. To say that the old content must go is to indicate that the old mind must die. Poet Tagore, in his book entitled *Stray Birds*, gives utterence to the feelings of a spiritual aspirant when he says :

Release me from my unfulfilled past, clinging
to me from behind, making death difficult.

It is unfulfilled psychological past that constitutes the content of the old mind. And it is this that clings from behind and does not allow the mind to be emptied of its past. The past all the time projects itself, and so even when new behaviour patterns have been shaped by the brain, under the impact of fresh and vital images, it is the content of the unfulfilled past which continues to inhabit them. While the new forms are needed, the problem of content cannot be left untouched. One may bring a mellowness in the otherwise harsh patterns and modes of action through the image-technique, but the old content is bound to raise its head sooner or later, What the old content does, even in the new forms, has been stated beautifully by Poet Tagore. He says :

Do not say 'It is morning' and dismiss it with a name of yesterday. See it for the first time as a new-born child that has no name.

The old content corrupts the new forms with its naming process. It uses the new patterns as a storehouse for old names. And a name contains the entire unfulfilled psychological past. When the old mind names what comes into the new forms then the past begins to pollute the fresh patterns of life. To build the new and fresh patterns and yet not to allow them to be polluted by the touch of the old content — it is this that is demanded of the spiritual aspirant. Let the road to communication proceed and carry the images, constructed consciously by thought and vitalised by emotion. Let the spiritual aspirant bless the onward journey of the images as they move along the path for the fulfilment of their mission – the forging of new modes of behaviour and action. But the spiritual pilgrim must move along the mountain path in search of the New Content with which to inspire the new forms which the image-technique will bring into existence. One can move along the mountain path only by shedding one's burden. One cannot move with all the burden along the steep path as by so doing one is bound to get out of breath. The images that go along the path of communication carry with them the designs and models of new patterns of behaviour. When the spiritual aspirant moves along the difficult mountain path with the heavy load of the old content then he realizes that he must become lighter so that his climb may be easier. The old content has to be carried upwards because thus alone it can be emptied. The process of becoming lighter and lighter ultimately results in complete emptying of the image in which the old content has been carried.

Before we proceed further along this road, it has to be remembered that any modification of habits happens within the campus of the old content. And so there is a change in structure but not in content by this process of modification. The modification of habit is done with the consent of the mind, and surely the mind can never give its consent for the issue of its own death-warrant. The image-building technique functions at the structural level so that new behaviour-patterns may come into being. These modes of action are likely, in their turn, to become new habits where the form is different but the content is the same. These new habits can be prevented from coming into existence if the forms are impregnated constantly with New Impulses. But if these impulses do not come then we will be caught again in the compulsions of new habits. The function of conscious image-building is to bring into existence new forms so that structural rigidities of habit may be removed, and fluid and pliable modes of behaviour may come into being. But if one is satisfied with mere modifications of habit then one will never know the joy of creative living. Into the exoteric forms, the esoteric wine must be poured, for, otherwise the changed forms will soon degenerate into hard and rigid expressional structures. Just as re-vitalization of brain is not sufficient unto itself, similarly modification of habits is not the journey's end. It has to be followed by the Transformation of the Mind. A New quality of mind must come into being for then only the modified forms will be inspired by a New Impulse, making one's life both structurally and spiritually significant.

In the process of habit-modification while the forms of habit-expression change, the craving of the mind remains. And it is the craving which is the content of the mind, it is the unfulfilled past clamouring for its fulfilment. The craving is the centre round which new circles of habit will be formed. Here the objects for habit fulfilment may be different, but the old craving continues. All modifications exist within the continuing background of the mind. The consciously built images break the monotony of habit, but not its craving. Now the forms of habit can be changed by one's efforts, but the craving cannot be eliminated by human endeavour. It is not by will-power that the craving can be wiped away, nor can it be done by the conscious image-building mechanism. As the Bhagavad Gītā says :

> The objects turn away when nourishment is denied to them, but still the relish or the craving remains, even the craving is dissolved when the Supreme is seen.

In this verse *Viṣaya* is the word used for objects. Now Viṣaya does not exist by itself, it is the creation of the mind. When mind projects its memory-content upon a thing or an idea or a person then it becomes a *Viṣaya*. Since it is the creation of the mind, when habit-modification takes place this *Viṣaya* is dissolved, but the craving of the mind remains, and it takes its habitat in new habit-forms. If this craving is not dissolved then there is every likelihood of the new modes of action, created by image-building mechanism, becoming a new house in which the content of the old mind can reside. It is said that when the Lord Buddha attained Buddhahood or Illumination the first statement that he made was 'I have seen you, O, Dweller of the house; I shall no longer allow you to occupy the house'. The Dweller of the house is the craving. Lord Buddha said that the cause of human suffering is *tanhā* or craving. But the above verse of the Bhagavad Gītā says that the relish or craving can be dissolved only when the Supreme is seen. How is one to see the Supreme ? So long as the craving is there, the Supreme cannot be seen, and without seeing the Supreme the craving cannot be dissolved. It is a curious paradox of spiritual life. How is one to resolve it ? Patañjali in the second sūtra of the Fourth Section of the *Yoga Sūtras* says :

> The birth of a new species or mutation
> is caused by the over-flow of nature.

Here he speaks not of the new species in the biological but in the psychological sense. Even biologically, a mutation is caused by evolutionary factors from above, to use the term coined by Dr. Raynor Johnson. He says in his book *Nurslings of Immortality* :

> When I survey the account which Darwinism and its derivatives give of the Evolution of living things from Protozoa to Homo Sapiens, I am bound to say that the two issues of Variation and Natural Selection, together with all the detailed knowledge which genetics is supplying, hold out great promise of accounting for the factors in Evolution which derive from below. I am equally clear that regarded as

the sole and sufficient basis of Evolution they are completely inadequate.

As we stated above, Dr. Raynor Johnson believes that an adequate explanation of evolution can be found only when we understand not only the factors from below, but also factors from above. Modern writers on the subject of Evolution have introduced the term 'internal selection' as a supplement to Natural Selection of Darwinism. In the book *Intelligence Came First* edited by E. Lester Smith we are told :

> The Darwinian theory is right as far as it goes but it is inadequate as a complete explanation of evolutionary events. An animal is free to select his environment and feeling habits. Another kind of internal selection in evolution may act directly upon mutations at the cellular level such that only those survive which are favourable to the internal coordination which is life.

Internal selection at the human level may function in a two-fold manner. One is the internal select on by the mind. This selection can result in modifications such as we have been discussing. Such modifications are within the sphere of mind's continuing background. Here one sees changes in structure retaining the same mental content. They help in bringing into existence flexible structures breaking down the rigidities of habitual forms. But there is another internal selection which is not of the mind, but belongs to factors that transcend the mind. They are of the nature of mutations, and, not mere modifications. But for these internal selections, either by the mind or by factors beyond the mind, one has to assign to consciousness a place of primary importance. Sir Alister Hardy in his book *The Biology of God* says :

> Darwinian evolution need no longer be considered an entirely materialistic doctrine. It can only be so regarded if we either deny the part played by conscious behaviour or deem consciousness itself to be no more than an illusory by-product

of an entirely mechanistic system. I maintain that there is no reasonable support for either view and that to proclaim them as part of well-established science is not only an unwarranted assumption but is most likely a misrepresentation of the nature of life and of man.

In the modern thinking on the subject of evolution, one notices a clear shift from a materialistic to a non-materialistic approach. In this shift we see movement from the material to the mental, from behaviour to consciousness, from Natural selection to Internal selection, from the determinism of Nature to freedom of the individual. This movement is yet exploratory, for, there is no clear distinction between the Internal selection of the conditioned consciousness, and the Internal selection of a free mind. In regard to discrimination there is a great deal of confusion. How can mind discriminate rightly when it is conditioned by its own background ? True discrimination dawns upon one's consciousness, it cannot be the product of the mind. The internal selection made by the mind is for the fulfilment of its unfulfilled past. It is this which forms the content of image-building whereby modifications in habit are sought to be brought about. We must move towards total freedom of the mind, for, it is only in that state that right selection or choice comes. When the new behaviour patterns are inspired by such right choice then we shall know what New Wine in New Bottles means. Then not only the forms will be new, the content too will be new. And the new content will not allow new habit formations. It will keep all behaviour patterns flexible and tentative so that no rigidity enters the field. When the flexible forms readily respond to the touch of the New Impulse then does one really know what it is to do the right thing, in the right manner and at the right time.

The path that leads to meditation demands the death of the old mind. We rise spiritually only as we stand on our dead selves. From the point of holding the consciously built images, the path bifurcates. There is one path for the transmission of images, and there is another path for the transcendence of

Images. The transcendence of images demands the death of the mind. Death is a classmate of meditation — not the death of the body but of the mind. It is not that first there must be the death of the mind and then comes meditation. As one explores the way of meditation there takes place simultaneously the death of the mind. J. Krishnamurti says in *Commentaries on Living* (First Series) :

> Right meditation is essential for the purgation of the mind, for without the emptying of the mind there can be no renewal. Mere continuity is decay.

As stated above "mere continuity is decay". One must make a distinction between decay and death. Decay is forcible imposition of discontinuity. It is forcible because it is brought about by circumstances. It brings into existence a state of weariness or dullness. But the mind that invites death has a different quality. It is this invitation to death which is the beginning of true meditation. In this death, the mind is emptied of all its content. Where death is, there alone can renewal be. When we speak of the Transformation of Mind we refer to the emergence of a New Mind. But the question is how does one come to the experience of mind's death, of the total purgation, of the emptying of all its content ? Can mind be consciously emptied ? Obviously it cannot be, for, a conscious emptying is only a state of modified continuity where the old is being substituted by something that is seemingly new. J. Krishnamurti says in the same book :

> There is freedom when the entire being, the superficial as well as the hidden, is purged of the past. Will is desire; and if there is any action of the will, any effort to be free, to denude oneself, then there can never be freedom, the total purgation of the whole being.

Thus the emptying of the mind can never happen by conscious effort. Then how does it come about ? If the mind cannot be emptied then can it empty itself ? If so, how ? If the mind has to be totally purged then why hold consciously created images and then take them up hill on the steep path to the summit ? What do we exactly mean when we talk of emptying the content of the mind ? Where does the content reside ? It obviously resides in the consciously created images. And so to empty the mind is to empty the images created by it, for, it is the image that contains mind's content. In creating and holding the image, the content of the mind is gathered, brought to a focus. This is necessary both for Transmission as well as Transcendence. The consciously created images are transmitted to the brain for processing modified patterns of behaviour. Similarly the consciously created images are taken along the path of communion where they get denuded. Both these processes must go on, for, thus alone the rhythm of Communion and Communication is maintained. It is in this rhythm that one can know what healthy and creatively rich spiritual life is.

The Old Mind and the New Mind cannot be mixed up, for, in so doing the Old will swallow the New, and that which remains is the ugly face of continuity. By such mingling, at best, what will come about is a modified continuity. But we want the modified behaviour patterns to be imbued with the New Impulse, not one that is adulterated with the old. H. P. Blavatsky says in *The Voice of the Silence* :

> Eternal life's pure waters, clear and crystal, with the monsoon tempest's muddy torrents cannot mingle. Heaven's dew-drop glittering in the morn's first sunbeam within the bosom of the lotus, when dropped on earth becomes a piece of clay; behold the pearl is now a speck of mire.

The New Impulse cannot mingle with the muddy stream of the Old Mind, and if it does, then the pearl will become a speck of mire. The old content must go totally, without any reserve. This content is the unfulfilled psychological memory. While the talent and the skill learnt by the mind must remain, the psychological past must be dissolved totally and completely. The mind must die to its old content before the stream of the New

Impulse, clear and crystal, can flow into it. H.P. Blavatsky says :

> One single thought about the past that thou hast left behind, will drag thee down and thou wilt have to start the climb anew. Kill in thyself all memory of past experiences. Look not behind or thou art lost.

One may ask : Does the way of meditation indicate to us as to how one can be totally free from the thoughts left behind ? The images that one carries along the mountain path hold in their womb the thoughts left behind, for, they contain the burden of mind's psychological memory. How to be free from it so that we can move along the path of the Transformation of the Mind ? It is this inquiry that invites us to enter the fascinating land of Meditation and to unravel its secrets and its mysteries.

FIFTEEN

THE WATCHER, BUT NOT THE WATCHMAN

THE subject of Meditation is very much in the air today all over the world, but for many people it is much more than that — it has become a live issue. Why is this so ? Why is the modern man turning so frantically to the way of meditation ? This is so because he wishes to get out of the tyranny of mind's opposites. We saw in the First Chapter that in any given situation, mind has only two ways of dealing with it. These two ways are — Struggle or Submission. The mind wants us to alternate between the two so that when one is tired of the struggle, one can move on to the alternative of submission. But these alternative movements have led us no where near the solution of our psychological problems of life. Man is consciously or unconsciously in search of the Third Way. Along this Third Way the opposites are not brought to a compromise, nor is a reconciliation sought to be arrived at. The Third Way is the way of Transcending the opposites which does not mean negating the opposites. It indicates a way wherein the opposites can co-exist at the same time. The simultaneous existence of the two is inconceivable for the mind. Time and space are the categorical imperatives of the mind without which it cannot function. And in time and space two things exist one after the other, and not at the same time and at the same place.

But how can the opposites exist together without cancelling each other. We have stated above that there is a transcendence of opposites without negating them. How can the opposites be negated without negating manifestation itself ? Surely manifestation exists by the operation of the opposites. Duality is the very nature of manifestation. In manifestation we are confronted with the problem of relationship. This is so because there is the existence of duality. After all, one can think of relationship only when there exist dualities. What then is meant by transcending the opposites without negating them ?

It is true that manifestation cannot be thought of without the existence of dualities. But the question is must these dualities be in conflict with each other ? Must they be mutually exclusive ? Or can they be complementaries to each other ? Must the dualities exist always as opposites, or is there the possibility of a new relationship between the two ? It is true that two contradictory things cannot exist together. But this is so when we look at them in a restricted sphere. When our perceptive sphere is enlarged then the two contradictory things can and do exist together. Light and shade cannot exist together in a restricted area of perception, but if we enlarge this perceptive range, for example in a landscape, then we find that light and shade do exist together, not only that, their co-existence gives to the landscape a beauty and a charm. In this larger perceptive sphere, the contradictories have been transformed into contraries. Paul Roubiczec in his deeply metaphysical book *Thinking in Opposites* says :

> Contradictory opposites become mere contrasts if we enlarge the sphere of our considerations. . . . Contrasts, on the other hand, become contradictory opposites when we restrict our attention.

Two contrasting things can co-exist, but two contradictory things cannot. In both cases the opposites are the same, but they are put in two differing backgrounds. If contradictories can be transformed into contrasts then they can remain together without cancelling each other. Philosophically speaking dualities can exist together if they are transformed into polarities. The North pole and the South pole do not cancel each other; they together enable the earth to exist in its orbit. The two opposite poles in an electrical circuit generate energy. But what must be the background in which the psychological dualities can co-exist without conflict and without cancelling each other ? It is obvious that the dualities can exist in perfect harmony only in the background of the non-dual experience. It is the non-dual which can contain within itself all dualities. If the Non-dual is the ground in which the Dual exists then the conflict of the opposites is over. Move away from the non-dual experience and you are once again caught in the battle of the opposites. It is in the Non-dual that the opposites are transcended without being negated. This is indeed the meaning of God, the Transcendent being at the same time Immanent. C. Jinarajadas in his little book *What We Shall Teach* expresses this idea beautifully. He says :

> By two stages men discover the One Lover . . . for He exists in a dual nature as the Immanence and the Transcendence. He is all that we see and hear and touch and smell and taste and think of and feel; yet is He at the same time none of these things. This is the mystery of His nature — He is the universe and yet is He other than the Universe.

It is in the experience of Transcendence, that Immanence becomes meaningful and significant. It is non-duality that imparts meaning to duality; it is Being that gives to Becoming a new dimension in which to function. He who has an experience of the Being is completely freed from the conflicts which otherwise appear in the field of Becoming. To search for the Being in the field of the mind is to engage oneself in an exercise of utter futility. Poet Rabindranath Tagore says in his book *Sadhana* :

> . . . if we do not see the Infinite Rest and only see the Infinite Motion, then existence appears to be a monstrous evil, impetuously rushing towards an unending aimlessness.

Infinite Rest is the Being even as Infinite Motion is the ceaseless movement of the Becoming. The Infinite Rest signifies the non-dual state, the state of Transcendence. And Infinite Motion denotes a condition of duality, the state of Immanence. The movement of duality will seem utterly aimless when the non-dual state is not perceived. The Non-dual contains all the opposites, and transforms them into polarities.

Man is today in a state of terrific inner conflict. He wants to solve these conflicts by making efforts on the plane of the Becoming; he wants to settle the problems of duality by remaining on the plane of duality. This effort is self-defeating, and so there is no wonder modern man is caught in the tyrannies and the compulsions of the mind. The wiser amongst us today have seen the futility of all efforts based on the plane of the opposites. It is they who have indicated the search for a New Way, for, the opposites can be contained only in the experience of the Non-dual. It is out of these indications that one sees a phenomenal interest in the subject of Meditation being evinced all over the world. Torn and tormented by the conflicts of the opposites, man is seeking the way of Transcendence. Needless to say — the way of Meditation is the way to the experience of the Non-Dual.

A pertinent question must arise: What is Meditation and how does it lead to the experience of the Non-Dual ? Does one carry with oneself the images consciously created and passionately held along this path ? If so, will not these images prove an obstacle in coming to the Non-Dual experience ? We must first understand what meditation is. Surely it is not sitting with closed eyes, taking a particular posture and engaging oneself in the exercises of breath control. One may do these things or one may not, for, they are not a part of meditation. Meditation is also not a repetition of some *mantra*, given by a guru or selected from some scriptural writings. Meditation is also not doing *pūjā* or ritualistic worship of some deity. Then what is meditation ? Is it a practice of concentration on some object or some idea ? J. Krishnamurti says in his *Freedom from the Known :*

> Meditation is not following any system; it is not constant repetition and imitation. Meditation is not concentration. It is one of the favourite gambits of some teachers of meditation to insist on their pupils learning concentration, that is, fixing the mind on one thought and driving out all other thoughts. ... It means that all the time you are having a battle between the insistence that you must concentrate on the one hand and your mind on the other which wanders away to all sorts of other things. ...When your mind wanders off it means you are interested in something else.

Today all types of meditation systems are being expounded and propagated. In some quarters meditation is being equated with the alpha-waves of the brain. In other quarters it amounts to fast and almost violent breathing and giving release, almost as violently as breathing, to animal urges of the body. There are some schools of meditation where the pupil has to do nothing but wait for the transmission of power or *Śakti* from the guru. In some systems of meditation complete emphasis is put on complex physical postures and intricate breathing exercises. There are systems of meditation in which one is engaged in elaborate ritualistic worship, sometimes associated with repetition of some mantras. Meditation is not an act of self-hypnosis, nor is it rendering the mind so passive that it can come easily under the hypnotic spell cast by the guru. There is much irrelevant stuff that has gathered round meditation with the result that confusion has been made more and more confounded. Unless all this confusion is discarded one cannot come to grips with the real problem of meditation.

One of the great misconceptions about meditation is that it is a process of deep thinking. It is believed that in order to meditate one must enter into a state of profound reflection. But the fact of the matter is — Meditation is not a process of thinking, not even the subtlest and the most abstract. After all the process of thinking keeps us moving in the circle of the known. This circle cannot be broken just because one engages oneself in abstruse thinking. All thinking is in a circle, and so by such a process one can never come to the discovery of the Third Way. And our urgent need is to find that way so that one can be free from the tyranny and the compulsions of mind's alternatives. Meditation is not a process of the stoppage of thought either. This is so because the thought process cannot be stopped by conscious effort. It is the conscious stoppage of thought which is concentration. But thought cannot be kept out or banished by any act of concentration even if a tremendous power of will is brought into operation. One can suppress a thought, but can never stop it. And a suppressed thought rebounds with tremendous force, taking the meditator almost unawares.

We have so far seen only what meditation is not, but then what after all is meditation ? Meditation is really an observation of the thought process. To observe the movement of thought is indeed the act of true meditation. This idea of observation, being the core and the crux of meditation, has come down to us from remotest times. One sees this in the Vedas and the Upaniṣads, and from there down to the present time. In the Ṛgveda and in the Upaniṣads, in the Muṇḍakopaniṣad and the Śvetāśvatara Upaniṣad particularly, we find the illustration of two birds, identical in form, like inseparable friends, sitting on the same branch of a tree, one eating the fruit and the other only watching the activity of the first bird. We are not going into the interpretation of this symbolism of the Two Birds. One thing is certain that since the illustration speaks of the Two Birds as identical and inseparable, the symbol speaks of only one entity that eats the fruit and also watches the eating process. The Witness and the Participant are not two different entities. To be a witness to one's own participation in life's process is being indicated by this illustration of the Two Birds, first appearing in the Vedas, and later reproduced in two of the major Upaniṣads.

The idea of the Witness and the Participant, at the same

time, and not one after the other, is to be found once again in the *Bhagavad Gītā* as also in the *Yoga Sūtras* of Patañjali. This is presented in the form of *Abhyāsa* and *Vairāgya* — the former denotes participation while the latter signifies being a witness. To observe one's act of participation, to witness mind in action — it is this which is placed before the aspirant as a technique of Yoga or Meditation. In all acts of participation, it is obvious that the mind or the thought process is involved. And so to observe one's own movement of thought in the midst of one's participation is the technique given to the aspirant, intent on pursuing the path of meditation.

One finds this observation technique greatly amplified in the Buddhist Way of Meditation. It is known as the *Vipassana* Meditation. This consists of a fourfold observation, namely of *Kāya*, Bodily movements, *Vedanā*, sensations of heat and cold felt by the body, *Citta*, the movement of thought, and *Bhāvanā*, content of one's ideals and aspirations. This fourfold observation is called the Way of Mindfulness. Bhikku Soma in his book *The Way of Mindfulness* says that,

> ... it is the objective way of viewing anything whatsoever. It reckons just what is present and stopping the garrulity of one's own mind, lets the objects speak for themselves and unfold their character.

In a discourse which the Lord Buddha gave at Kammasadamma, a market-town of Kuru people, he said :

> This is the only way, O bhikkus, for the purification of beings, for the overcoming of sorrow and lamentation, for the destruction of suffering and grief, for reaching the right path, for the attainment of Nibbana, the four Arousings of Mindfulness.

From this one can see how the fourfold observation was regarded by the Buddha in the Yoga and Meditation sādhanā or discipline. The same approach in the field of Meditation is seen in Zen Buddhism. The Zen Master poses a problem before the disciple in the form of a Koan which is a paradoxical statement. The disciple is asked to solve it. He struggles with his mind but is unable to resolve it. Through Koan the disciple is asked to observe the movement of thought with reference to the problem posed by the Master. If he really observes this movement then he is sure to realize that the mind has no solution to it. There comes an awareness of the limitation of the mind. In the traditional Buddhist Way, one begins by observing one's breath and then moves on to body, to sensations, to thought and finally to ideals and aspirations. This fourfold observation, in terms of Mindfulness, has the same purpose, namely, to know the ways of the mind by closely observing its movements. Thus both in Hinduism and in Buddhism we find this Observation technique suggested as part of Yoga and Meditation practices.

One may ask: What is the purpose of this observation ? It has a twofold purpose. One, to lay bare the content of the mind, and two, to empty that content. The emptying is possible only when the content is not only observed but brought to a focus. This is what observation does in the first instance. But in the process of observation one has first to deal with intruding and unwanted thoughts. This is the main problem of meditation, too. When we sit in meditation, taking a particular thought or idea for reflection, the first thing that happens is the onrush of unwanted thoughts. To keep out these intruding thoughts is the most difficult thing, for, if one resists their arrival then they get strengthened; and if one gives way to them then one is carried away by them. Neither resistance nor indulgence helps us to deal with the cowans and intruders that disturb our meditation constantly. In fact, there is no rest or respite from them with the result that our usual meditation is a ceaseless battle against the encroachments of these unwanted thoughts. They are like squatters who cannot be dislodged from their unauthorised occupations. Arjuna expressed this very difficulty before Lord Krishna, and then the Lord gave him the simple formula of *Abhyāsa* and *Vairāgya*, of observation in the midst of action or participation. Thus observation technique has been suggested by our ancient teachers for dealing effectively with intruding thoughts. In this observation the motives and the intentions of the mind are laid bare. And it is thus that they become amenable for clear and sustained observation.

Among the modern thinkers, three most outstanding among them, Sri Ramana Maharshi, Sri Aurobindo and J. Krishnamurti, have placed before the spiritual aspirants the same approach of Observation for dealing with intruding and unwanted thoughts. Not a control of mind by resistance, but quieting the mind through observation, it is this which these modern thinkers have expounded while speaking about Meditation. H. P. Blavatsky in her *Voice of the Silence* says :

> The ripple of effect, as the great tidal wave,
> thou shalt let run its course.

To allow the circumstances to run their course is to ask the tidal wave of thought to play out its game unhindered. In order to be free from mental intruders to ask them to run their course is the advice given by H. P. Blavatsky to spiritual aspirants. To allow the tidal wave of thought to run its course is to refrain from interfering, in its movement. Not to interfere with its course is just to observe its movement. Patañjali also defines *Dhyāna* or Meditation as an act of observing the flow of thought without any interruption. We see here the same observation technique about which we have been discussing, for dealing effectively with the intruding thoughts. Sri Ramana Maharshi in one of his talks given in 1936 says :

> After the camphor burns away no residue is left. The mind is the camphor.

To allow the camphor to burn away is similar to the tidal wave being allowed to run its course. If the mind is allowed to run its course then no residue of thought remains. The intruding thoughts leave no trace behind if they are not resisted but are observed as one would observe a procession without any interruption or interference.

In the writings of Swami Vivekananda we find a clear instruction given to the student of Yoga wherein he says that one should stand back from one's thoughts, allow them to occur in one's mind as they will, and observe them to find out as to what they are. This is like allowing the camphor to burn itself away or like the tidal wave being allowed to run its course.

But among the modern thinkers Sri Aurobindo and J. Krishnamurti have not only been clearest regarding the technique of observation, they have also given detailed instructions about this technique. In observation there are many issues involved, such as, What to observe ? When to observe ? Where to observe ? But above all How to observe ? It is in regard to the question of How to observe that we have very clear indications given to us by these two thinkers. We shall first consider the question : How to observe ? and then turn to the other questions what, when and where. We have already considered the question : Why to observe ? in the earlier part of this chapter. Observation is necessary in order to deal with intruding thoughts which cannot be tackled by the usual processes of concentration. And without dealing with the intruding thoughts we cannot come to the emptying of the mind which is needed for the death of the Old Mind and the emergence of the New Mind. Here we are concerned with the question : How to observe ? This question obviously includes the inquiry as to what after all is observation. We are taking up the question of How to observe first because it directly impinges upon the problem of how to deal with the intruding thoughts. And this is the most practical aspect in relation to Meditation. We will be able to turn to the other three questions more easily — the What, the When and the Where — if we first explore this fundamental question : How to observe ?

In this connection the following words of Sri Aurobindo are of great help. He says :

> If thoughts and activities come, they cross the mind as a flight of birds crosses the sky in a windless air. It passes, disturbs nothing, leaving no trace. ... Even if a thousand images or the

> most violent events pass ac oss, the calm stillness remains as if the very texture of the mind were a substance of eternal and indestructible peace.

Here Sri Aurobindo tells us about the state of the mind under the impact of intruding thoughts. He says that these thoughts may come and go without leaving any trace and without causing any disturbance to the stillness of the mind. But our experience is that these thoughts do not just come and go — they linger, many times they settle down, and even when they depart they leave their traces behind which become the centres of psychological memory. How to induce thoughts to come and go leaving no mark behind ? It is this which raises the question : How to observe ? Sri Aurobindo asks us :

> ... to look at the thoughts as not one's own, to stand back as the witness — the thoughts are regarded as things coming from outside, and they must be felt as if they were passers-by crossing the mind-space with whom one has no connection and in whom one takes no interest.

We are asked to display the Wayfarer's attitude towards the intruding thoughts, treating them as strangers and therefore refusing to call out any mental or emotional involvement or even interest in their activities. Sri Aurobindo speaks of still another way in the following words :

> There is an active method by which one looks to see where the thoughts come from, one can detect them coming, then before they enter, they have to be thrown away.

Here Sri Aurobindo suggests the way of the watchman. If as an alert watchman we can detect the arrival of the intruding thoughts, hear their silent footsteps, then such thoughts will not dare to intrude. Seeing the Watchman these intruding thoughts will hide themselves somewhere, and so they will not disturb. Whether one acts like a Witness or a Wayfarer or a Watchman, the question still remains as to how is this to be done; what is the *modus operandi* for playing these roles when the attack of the intruding thoughts comes. The mind is a very clever entity and therefore rises to all occasions to safeguard its interests. It has a great urge to live and therefore fights death on all the fronts. In playing the above-mentioned three roles, it divides itself into two—calling one the lower, and, other the higher. The three-fold role is taken over by the Higher Mind implying that it will control the lower by these processes. When this happens then the three roles become meaningless—in fact, the very purpose of these roles is defeated. Then the higher mind sits in judgment over the lower putting on the robes and the regalia of either the Witness or the Wayfarer or the Watcher. Then what is one to do ? Perhaps the following words of J. Krishnamurti, appearing in his book *Freedom from the Known* may help us to break this deadlock :

> Meditation is to be aware of every thought and of every feeling, never to say it is right or wrong but just to watch it and move with it. In that watching you begin to understand the whole movement of thought and feeling. And out of this awareness comes silence ... this silence is meditation in which the meditator is entirely absent, for the mind has emptied itself of the past.

There is a difference between watching the arrival of intruding thoughts, and welcoming the arrival of such thoughts, between the role of the watchman and the watcher. The disturbing thoughts should be induced to come so that one can observe all their movements. It is like inviting these thoughts and asking them to tell their story. The intruding thoughts must be induced to talk and in such talking tell their story without any fear of interruption. It is a well known fact that modern psychiatrists, in dealing with their mental patients, are concerned about inducing the latter to talk or to come out. If these patients can come out with their stories then the doctors say that more than half the battle is won. In this very talking the pent-up feelings of the patients find a release. In the same way the mind must be induced to talk so that it relates its story without any inhibition whatsoever.

If one could observe the movement of the mind without any judgment, if one could listen to the story of the mind without any evaluation, then in that observation and in that listening the mind will become quiet. Having told the story its chattering automatically ceases. The mind becomes quiet, it has not to be quietened. But the question is : Will not the Higher and the Lower mind come into existence even in this act of observation or the act of listening ? How can this be prevented, for, if any judgment or evaluation comes then the mind will refuse to unfold its story. There will be nothing to observe when evaluation and judgment enter the field of observation. Once again the question is; what is one to do ?

It has to be remembered that the observation of or the listening to the mind cannot be done by shutting oneself behind closed door and making a firm effort to observe the movement of the mind. The moment one shuts oneself up in a room, that very moment the mind also shuts its movements down. The mind can be observed only in motion. Only in the mirror of one's daily life can mind be observed. J. Krishnamurti says :

> So Meditation can take place when you are sitting in a bus or walking in the woods full of light and shadows, or listening to the singing of birds or looking at the face of your wife or child.

It is in extensive awareness that the observation of mind is possible, never in an act of exclusive awareness. Without interrupting one's activities even for a minute, one can do this observation. It is in exclusive awareness that the division of the higher and the lower mind comes into existence. If while observing the mind in action there takes place a division of the higher and the lower, then either action stops or observation itself stops. This is an indication that in the act of observation the evaluator has entered. J. Krishnamurti says that in real meditation, the meditator is entirely absent. It is the meditator that is the judge and the evaluator. For the elimination of the division of the Higher and the Lower, extensive awareness is the only way.

In the matter of dealing with the intruding thoughts, one may begin with the action of the Wayfarer and move on to play the role of the Witness, and thence come to the detecting device of the Watchman While these three stages are necessary in the act of observing one's thoughts, one must finally come to the role of the watchman, who is not concerned with the throwing away of the intruders, but in quietly watching their movements with total alertness so that in the performance of his duties he is extensively aware. The subject of Extensive Awareness has been discussed by the author in his two previous books — *The Nameless Experience* (Second edition published by Motilal Banarsidass, Delhi) and *Yoga — the Art of Integration* (published by the Theosophical Publishing House, Adyar, Madras). As the subject has been discussed exhaustively in the two above-mentioned books, it would be unnecessary to repeat whatever has been said there regarding the question of Extensive Awareness. As this very phrase indicates, in this awareness, there is no exclusion of thoughts, but inclusion of all thoughts. Here the very term 'intruder' is elimitated. No thought is an intruder. What we call as an intruder is also a part of mind's landscape. It is when the perspective range is restricted that a thought becomes an intruder. But if the range is widened, then the so-called intruder becomes a part of the whole landscape. Not only that, the presence of the so-called intruding thought gives to the landscape a perspective by which the whole scene becomes living, not flat and dull as would be the case otherwise.

The secret of Extensive Awareness lies in the fact that in it there is not the slightest trace of resistance or resentment. Besides, in extensive awareness there arises no possibility of the division of the mind into the higher and the lower, for, both are included in its range of awareness. While introducing the question: How to observe, we mentioned that there are three other questions associated with it — they are what to observe, where to observe and when to observe. The subject of extensive awareness will become clear as we briefly examine these three questions.

It may be said that the question, What to observe, has no relevance after all that we have discussed in this chapter. We have again and again stated with reference to the fourfold role of the Wayfarer, the Witness, the Watchman and the Watcher, that there must be the observation of thought with all its movements. But the word *thoughts* is rather vague and slippery. Thought can be observed only in terms of the form and shape that it takes. This is the Image. In Extensive Awareness too we are concerned with the observation of mental images. We have discussed in the earlier chapters that transmission of images to the brain loses its effectiveness if the images are not clear and vivid, and also if an element of indulgence is introduced in the holding of the images. In Indulgence the energy of the image is frittered away and so the impact on the brain of such images is very weak. In such a condition it is the habitual image that holds mastery over the consciously created new images. Because of indulgence in image-building, the brain is induced to go on with habitual behaviour-patterns, and is not persuaded to bring any modification in their modes of expression. Similarly the images moving upwards, after the point of bifurcation, towards the summit of Communion, refuse to move if an element of resistance is introduced. Images consciously created and held with emotional involvement move along the transmission line to the alert and activised brain for bringing into existence modified patterns of behaviour. This is a movement towards the fields of communication. But without the New Impulse coming from communion these new modes of behaviour are like new bottles containing the old wine. And so there has to be a search for the New Impulse. This search demands the emptying of the mind of all its old content. And the old content lies in the consciously created and passionately held images. If they are to be divested of the old content the images and their expressional behaviour have to be observed. And so the mountain path, leading to communion, has to start from the point of observation. Here one must observe the consciously created images and their manifold movements. One must listen to the story of the old content as narrated by the images. But let even a subtle factor of resistance, or resentment come in and the images will refuse to carry on their narration. No indulgence in images along the path of communication, and no resistance to the narrations of the images along the path of Communion — this is the twofold requirement to be followed by the spiritual aspirant. It means no indulgence along the downward path, and no resistance along the upward path. But what does the observation of mental images signify ? What is it that one observes ?

Images are full of the stories of the old content. In fact, they are vibrant with all the memories that the old mind has stored up and which it wants to live again and again. To observe one's thoughts is to observe these images with all their movements, in fields near and far. It is an act of listening to what the images wish to say. But for this there must come into being a new relationship with our mental images. At present we hardly observe the images and we rarely listen to what they wish to say. We ask the images to shut themselves up as soon as they begin to unfold their story. There is an element of resistance, may be overt or it may be covert. The images immediately realize that their talk is not welcome. If its movements are regarded as intruders then there is not the right relationship between ourselves and the mental images. If one looks at the images with a sense of superiority then the images close down their shops so that we find that there is nothing to observe. Like a little child, the images have to be cajoled and persuaded to talk. It is this question of persuasion that brings us to the inquiry which we posed earlier, namely, when should one observe the images ?

It is obvious that flat and weak images will not reveal any content of the old mind. Such images have no energy to talk. A mere thought-image will not serve our purpose if we want the entire content of the old mind to be laid bare. The thought images must be charged with emotional involvement if we are to persuade them to talk. Thus, only vivid and emotionally charged images can give us indications as to what is the nature of the content of the old mind. It is only in the movement of the consciously created and passionately held images that meaningful observation is possible. And with such images there must not enter any resistance in the act of observation or in the act of listening. We must listen to the 'live broadcast' of the images for thus alone can we pick up the subtle nuances contained in their expressions.

When we begin to observe these clear and emotionally charged images then there emerges from them a procession of thought-images. These may be of all types of shapes and colours, pleasant as well as unpleasant. If we look at this procession without resistance or resentment then the procession moves, bringing in its train many strange images. If we resist or are resentful then the procession will stop, and the story of the images will remain untold. In such a state the procession will seem endless. But if we allow the procession to move on, look at it with tremendous interest but with no involvement then it will soon end. In the ending of the procession the story of the image will also come to an end with reference to that particular subject matter round which the conscious image-building had been done. To the question — When to observe ? the answer is : When the images have been emotionally charged and when they have been persuaded to talk and to move due to the approach, free from resistance and resentment.

We have seen that to observe the movement of thought is to observe the movement of the consciously built images with emotional intensity inhabiting them. With regard to the question of, When to observe ? we have seen that the best time to observe them is when they have been persuaded to talk and to move due to the absence of resistance and resentment. The third question which we had posed was : Where to observe ? When the emotionally vibrant images have been persuaded to unfold their story then they can be observed everywhere — in our activities and in our rest, in all that we do, in our reactions to the impacts of life, in the way we talk and also in the way we listen to others. These images jump about so much that they cannot be contained at one place. Thus it is not difficult to observe these images since they are all-pervading. In terms of all these various questions — the Why, the What, the When, the Where and the How — we have covered the entire sphere of observation.

We saw that in this un-interrupted observation of mental images and their movements, in listening to their story without any resistance or resentment, the images get totally denuded of their entire content. The images are completely emptied of the content which the mind had stored in terms of psychological and associative memory. The mind is emptied of the past, but one may ask : Is this all ? Is emptying the mind of its past content the culmination of meditation ? If so, is this not utterly negative ? The mind has been emptied of the past, but where is the New Impulse with which to inspire new behaviour-patterns and new modes of action ? In the very telling of its story the Image becomes quiet, but what next ? The death of the Old Mind has taken place, but where is the emergence of the New Mind ? Having dealt with the negative aspect of meditation, we shall turn to the positive experience of meditation in the next chapter. If the images have been denuded of the past content, where will the New Impulse arrive ? Is the role of the image over, or does it get transformed into a new receptacle to receive the refreshing waters of the New Impulse. We must turn to this positive aspect of Meditation as we carry on our inquiry further in the next chapter.

SIXTEEN

THE MYSTERIOUS EVENT

IT has been very often asked that if the mind is divested of all its content and rendered totally empty, will it not be extremely vulnerable where it will be exposed to all types of influences, good and bad. How can one be certain that in the empty mind will come only good influences which will give a New Impulse to the modified patterns of behaviour and modes of action ? It may become a hunting ground for undesirable influences as well. If this happens then the path leading to the emptiness of mind is much too dangerous. It may take the spiritual aspirant down, along an inclined plane. It is true that an empty mind is vulnerable, for, all its shelters are broken down and therefore lives under the open sky. But strange though it may sound, this vulnerability itself is its security. Its greatest protection lies in the fact that it has nothing to protect or defend. But how is one to be sure that it will not be invaded by forces that are unpleasant and undesirable ?

In order to understand this question one has to comprehend clearly the distinction between the mind that has been emptied, and the mind that has emptied itself. There is an emptiness with a centre and there is an emptiness without a centre. When the mind is sought to be emptied by a conscious effort then there continues to exist, in such a mind, a centre round which experiences are gathered. It is the centre that attracts influences from outside towards itself. Now in this centre lies the seed of the past content. In consciously emptying the mind one can remove the leaves and the branches and even the trunk of the tree, but if the seed remains then new sprouts are bound to come and another tree, the same or with some modifications, will burst forth to take the place of the old. Patañjali in the First Section of his *Yoga Sūtras* says in sūtra number fifty that :

> When there is a centre the impressions clinging to that centre will prevent new light from dawning upon the consciousness.

What is this centre ? Obviously it is the Motive. So long as the motive persists, so long there is emptiness with a centre. This motive is the centre maintained by the continuing entity which is the 'I'. This continuing entity projects itself in numerous ways, it puts on regalia to suit every occasion. It may change its regalia, but the entity that wears the regalia is the same. In the conscious emptying of the mind it is the regalia that is dropped, but the wearer of the regalia continues. In such emptying the effort is dropped but the effort-maker remains. It is the 'I' that constitutes the continuing centre of consciousness. And so in its seeming emptiness there is the centre which invites the old content to come in with a changed name so that its oldness may not be detected. The centre asks the old content to come back in a new attire. And so those ugly tendencies of the old content are brought back. In such emptiness there is no vulnerability, there is a centre through which the mind seeks to be invulnerable. To be vulnerable is to be free totally and completely from any vestige of the centre. Where man seeks to be invulnerable, he safeguards the centre even while he endeavours to come to seeming emptiness. The house that has been emptied is a haunted house for there is the lingering presence of one who has left in order to come back. The mind that has been emptied is not an empty mind.

In Zen Buddhism an incident has been narrated which says that when Bodhidharma, the founder of Zen Buddhism, went from South India to China, he was called by the Emperor. As he was a learned man, the Emperor asked him a question. The Emperor asked : "What is the first principle of Righteousness', to which Bodhidharma replied by saying, "Vast emptiness with nothing holy in it'. This statement clearly indicates the state of emptiness without a centre. There must be not even a centre of mind's holiness. The emptiness with a centre is arrived at by a process of conscious negation. But this is not enough, for, even the negator has to be negated. How can this be done consciously ? How can 'I' be removed by any effort of the 'I' ? The 'I' is the continuing centre and so whatever it does must be to perpetuate itself or to maintain its continuity undisturbed. It may modify its expressional continuity, but the centre of such modification is still the continuing entity. And yet without this state of unqualified emptiness, one cannot come in contact with the New Impulse with which to vitalise the modes of one's actions. J. Krishnamurti very often says 'It is the empty cup that can be filled'. The great Chinese philosopher, Lao Tze in his *Tao-Teh-King* says :

Thirty spokes surround one nave,
The usefulness of the Wheel is always
In that empty innermost.
You fashion clay to make a bowi,
The Usefulness of the bowl is always
In that empty innermost.
You cut out doors and windows to make a house,
Their usefulness to a house is always
In their empty space.

One can say with equal emphasis that the usefulness of the mind lies in the empty space that comes into being. Without this empty space the mind, with its thought process moves round and round in a circle. It relegates man to a stagnant existence where one can go on changing pictures painted on the wall — but still it is the wall of a prison house. Nothing fresh can enter one's psychological life so long as the wall remains. And if one's psychological life is stagnant then the physical life too must share the same fate. Sri Aurobindo says :

> It is clear that mind has not been able to change human nature radically. You can go on changing human institutions infinitely and yet the imperfections will break through all your institutions.

Human mind can at best bring about modifications, it cannot introduce fundamental transformation. It is outside the range and capacity of the mind. And so unless the mind is rendered mindless one cannot get out of the psychological stalemate in which one gets caught. To make mind, mindless is to empty it of all its content. Annie Besant says in her book *The Laws of Higher Life* :

> Just in proportion as we empty ourselves of all that we have, is there room for the Divine fullness to flow in, and fill us more than we were ever filled before.

Within the mind, space has to be created, for, otherwise the Divine Fullness cannot enter. It is in the creation of this space that the mind has to be emptied of all its content. It is generally believed that in order to lead a spiritual life, one must live from the centre. But life from the centre is only a modified continuity, whereas spirituality demands the living of a life that is radically different, not a mere difference in degree, but a difference in kind. Spirituality indicates the birth of a new psychological species. This cannot be if the mind retains its centre and discards only the superstructure. The very centre must go ere the birth of a New Mind can take place.

We have discussed in these pages that mind cannot be emptied; it can empty itself. All that one can do is to help the mind in the process of emptying itself. But this demands a new relationship with our mind. We must evoke a sense of confidence in the mind so that it can come out readily with all that it has to say. It has to be persuaded to do this because of an unfriendly relationship that exists today between us and our minds. How is this to be done ? We stated in the last chapter that this can be done by the process of observation. But it must be an observation done by a friend and not by a critic; it must be the observation of a watcher and not that of a watchman. The observation of a Witness or a Wayfarer is much too cold and impersonal; and the observation by a watchman is full of doubt and suspicion. We have suggested that the observation must be by the watcher. We must qualify this by saying that it must be by a friendly watcher. The watching must be done by love and affection even as the mother watches the child. There must be in this observation neither indifference nor interference, but a real, friendly interest. This new relationship with the mind is a very delicate affair, for, it can get disturbed in no time.

One may ask what could be the factor of disturbance in this new and friendly relationship with the mind ? It can be caused by even the slightest resistance or resentment. We have seen that the observation has to be of the mental images which contain the entire content of the old mind. The images have not only to be clear but also emotionally vivid. When these images are being observed, one will find that they are eager to tell their story, for, they are so full of it. And the story-telling comes to a focus when the emotionally charged images are held with intensity and at the same time with tenderness. One can tenderly play about with these images while they are being held. In this playful mood the images will begin to narrate their story. The images will relate their story without any inhibition because of the playful atmosphere that has been created. While telling the story, there will emerge numerous side-images. It is when this happens that no element of resistance or resentment must enter. The side-images may seem irrelevant or they may appear provocative. They will tend to break up our closely-guarded self-image, for, the story revealed by the Images is our own story. They unfold the contents of our own self-image. For the first time we are beginning to see ourselves as we are, without the mask of self-image. If we could listen to the biography of our self-image during this act of observation with interest, but without indifference or interference, then we shall know ourselves without any subterfuge, with all our motives revealed before our gaze. We shall be able to see our face in the biographical mirror placed before us by the Images. As they pass on, detail after detail of our life with all the motives, overt and covert, will be laid bare before us. If there is no resistance or resentment then the whole biographical narration of the self-image will be completed. The self-image will be emptied of all its content, and in this the mind too will empty itself of all that it has. The content of the mind and the content of the self-image are not two different things. When the self-image is unmasked then the content too is emptied. It is in the interest of protecting the self-image that we do not want the content of the mind to be laid bare. The content is the self-image — it is the 'I' or the *asmitā* of Patañjali. It is when the self-image is being unfolded that one recoils from it — but this recoiling is itself a factor of resistance and resentment. On the screen of observation let the pictures of the self-image be cast. The procession that emerges from the image is our own Procession — the procession of ourselves in a variety of robes and regalia, in a diversity of events and situations. When the story of the self-image is fully narrated then there is nothing for the mind to say. It has emptied itself and therefore has become silent. It is the coming of this silence which is meditation. A deep silence descends upon the mind, when the content of the self-image has been emptied. The mind has been rendered mindless; it is now a vessel which is clean and empty, ready to receive whatever is poured into it. This silence is not the product of the mind; it has come to the mind when the self-image has been emptied of all its content. J. Krishnamurti says in his *Freedom from the Known* :

> Silence put together by thought is stagnation, is dead, but the silence that comes when thought has understood its own beginning, the nature of itself... this silence is meditation.

It is said that self-knowledge is the beginning of wisdom. Surely the story of self-image revealed in the act of observation is indeed self-knowledge in its real nature. It is knowledge of ourselves as we are, not as we think we are, nor as we think we ought to be. In listening to our own story as narrated by the Images, we are freed from all our bondage to the past. We have been rendered innocent as a child, bereft of all our content which we had guarded so zealously by building stronger and stronger defence-mechanisms.

But is Meditation only a series of negations ? Does the path of ascent end at the summit of negation ? It is true that in the act of observation, that which is revealed by the images gets dropped and therefore negated. It is in this process of negation that the mind empties itself, it is totally denuded of all that it contained. But is negation the only fruit of ascent ? One is reminded of the words of Aśvapati as expressed by Sri Aurobindo in the great epic poem entitled *Savitri*. Coming to the Journey's end this King of the Madra country says :

> Only the everlasting NO has neared
> But where is the Lover's everlasting YES ?

Aśvapati utters these words, standing on the summit of total negation. In Meditation one does near the everlasting NO, but is there no everlasting YES of the Lover ? As the process of negation comes to an end, there descends upon the mind a deep and mysterious silence. Here, one may pause and consider as to whether the Journey of negation ever ends. Can one sit back comfortably having achieved a totality of negation ? If one sits back comfortably then that very state will have to be negated. The process of negation is a continuing process, it is like the mirror gathering dust which has to be blown off again and again. If the dust is allowed together then the mirror can be of no use whatsoever as it will not be able to reflect in a clear and undistorted manner. Similarly the process of negation has no end. If it ends then a new self-image will be formed with all the associated happenings. Must there always be a self-image through which one acts ? Cannot man face life directly without a mask ? It is only in a direct contact with life that one can receive the refreshing impluse with which to vitalise the modes and patterns of behaviour. The creation and maintenance of self-image is bound to cause strain and tension in one's psychological life. It is only the man who acts directly, not motivated by self-image that can initiate fresh mental images to activise the brain along new lines of expression. When self-image intervenes then man ceases to live, it is the self-image that lives and acts. We are not talking of modifying the self-image but the total elimination of it. When this happens then life is lived from moment to moment and not in terms of the unfulfilled past or the anticipated future. The self-image struts about so long as it is not exposed to full view. When the mask is removed or gets removed then where is the self-image ? When one knows what one really is or what one actually is, then there begins a movement of becoming which is natural, not cultivated as is the case when we live under the compulsions of the self-image. In the act of observation, which we have been discussing with reference to the subject of meditation, the images that are perceived are but the expressions of the one self-image which has been created and nourished by us. The images that we observe are not some out-side entities, they are part and parcel of the self-image. It is no use fighting against individual images, for, when the King-image, which is the self-image, vanishes then the other images wither away in no time.

In Ṛg Veda there is the story of Indra being approached by the gods for protection against the *asuras* or the dark forces. In reply to this appeal, Indra replies by saying that he will not waste his energies in destroying the *Paṇis* meaning small fry; he will destroy *Vṛtrāsura* the main cause of all trouble. The meaning of the word *Vṛtrāsura* is, one that casts a covering and thereby creates darkness. It is because of this darkness that the small fry are able to engage themselves in annoying tactics. But if the creator of darkness is destroyed then what can these small disturbers do ? This is exactly the case of the self-image and the numerous small images that cause continual disturbance to us. These images have no independent existence; they are the products and the off-shoots of the self-image.

Strange though it may sound, self-image dies of exposure. It cannot stand being exposed to outer gaze, it sustains itself only in concealment. It is the mask that protects it, for, under the mask it is able to hide its face. In the vivid and emotionally charged images it rejoices. But when the procession of these images is observed, without resistance or resentment, then gradually its face is revealed. The more the procession moves the more it is exposed. When the procession ends, its exposure, through a particular image-window, is complete. As this observation becomes a continuing process the self-image gets totally exposed, all its hiding places get demolished. No place is left to rest its weary feet.

In our usual endeavour to lead a spiritual life, we get staggered by the prospect of dealing with so many of our vices and weaknesses. It is this that sometimes causes disappointment to the neophyte. And so we spend days and nights fighting against these many weaknesses ... and we find that no end seems to be in sight. In this we waste our time and energy fighting the small fry. And the small fry have a tendency to rapidly multiply themselves, so that if we have dealt with some of them, many more spring up to take their places. To fight image after image is exactly the action of this nature. Instead of that if we watch without resistance these various images, then they show us the hiding places of the self-image. Thus does the self-image get completely exposed, and it is this exposure that causes its death.

But what is meant by the death of the self-image ? It means that the image has been transformed into a symbol. There is a gulf of difference between the Image and the Symbol. The image is filled with the projections of the mind. What we call the 'I' and take great pains to protect it, is but the product of the mind. It has been put together by the mind. This is indeed the *asmitā* of Patañjali. While the image is filled with mind's projections, the symbol is emptied of all projections. While the image is opaque, the symbol is transparent. It is the conveyer of light, for, there is nothing to block the passage of light. The symbol casts no shadow, for, it retains nothing. It serves as a clear and undistorting medium for the intimations that come from beyond the mind. That which was so far an Image has been transformed into a Symbol. It is through the Symbol that the positive experience can come to human consciousness. The symbol is verily a vessel, clean and empty, into which the New Impulse can be poured. The vessel has to be both empty and clean. If the mind is sought to be emptied, then such emptiness contains the touch of the entity that has sought to do the emptying. It is this touch which makes the vessel dirty. When the mind empties itself then there is no touch of such an entity. The symbol is a clean and an empty vessel. Sri Aurobindo says :

> The cup has to be left clean and empty for the Divine liquor to be poured into it. ... You must keep the temple clean if you wish to install there the Living Presence.

In the temple of life if there is an installation of only an idol, then one will be merely in the realm of Images — the realm of the self-image. It is in the transformation of the Image into a Symbol that the cup of consciousness is rendered clean and empty. It is to this transformation that Sri Aurobindo gives the name of the Over-mind, for, he says in his *Letters on Yoga :*

> ... the Overmind is the passage through which one passes from Mind to super-mind.... Th Over-mind has a great plasticity and is a field of multiple possibilities.

It is this state of Over-mind where there takes place the transformation of an image into a symbol. The symbol has multiple possibilities because it has nothing of its own. It is only a passage, absolutely clear and unhindered, which allows the Impulses of the Beyond to enter human consciousness. While the emptying of the image is a negative process, the symbol carrying the New Impulse is a positive experience. The Void indeed is the Plenum, but it has to be a void without a centre. Between such a Void and the Plenum there is no time-lag; they are a simultaneous phenomena. And because the symbol is completely transparent, it has multiple possibilities. The symbol is like what Patañjali says in the First Section of his *Yoga Sūtras*. It is said in Sūtra 41 :

> In the case of one whose reactive tendencies have been eliminated, there arises a fusion of the knower, the known and the knowledge even as the transparent jewel gets fused with the colour of the surface on which it rests.

The symbol is like the transparent jewel where all differences have fused into one another creating a non-dual state. Thus in the transformation of the image into a symbol there comes the culminating experience of Meditation. It is in the non-dual state, and there alone, that one comes to the supreme experience, of Meditation. Meditation is an intensely positive experience, not an affirmative experience of the Mind. Generally mind's affirmations are regarded by us as something positive. The assertion of the mind has no positive character in it. It is only the negative film that can take a positive photograph. In the transformation of the Image into a Symbol there comes into being a total negativity of consciousness. Into this pours the New Wine with which to vitalise one's daily life. The negativity of consciousness represents man's ascent into the realms which touch the field of meditation. When the New Impulse is poured into this negativity then there takes place the miracle of descent. Without such descent, the experience of meditation has no validity.

When the self-image is negated totally and without any reserve then there comes to one a vision of one's true self. It is the vision of Reality, of Truth, or of Beauty. It is here that one sees one's *Svarūpa*, one's Being. But the vision of one's Fullness, which the Being is, has such dynamism that one cannot but burst out in a new process of Becoming, in the supreme act of *Svadharma*. In the light of the Being whatever one does is *Svadharma* containing the very quality of Being itself. In the real becoming which is *Svadharma* there is a naturalness and therefore no frustration whatsoever. When life is lived in terms of *Svadharma* then there is an experience of Creative Joy from moment to moment. It is this *Svadharma* which imparts fresh vitality to all modes of action and behaviour. In the total negation of the self-image there descends upon one's consciousness deep and profound silence. In this silence is heard the Voice, the Voice of the silence. Then it is this voice that commands, not the puny will of the mind. Its commands will create fresh and vital images with which to energise the brain for ever-new modes of action and behaviour. About this action emanating from the Silence, Sri Aurobindo says :

> A mind that has achieved this calmness can begin to act, even intensely and powerfully, but it will keep its fundamental stillness, originating nothing from itself but receiving from Above and giving it a mental form without adding any thing of its own.

In terms of this Voice of the Silence, the mind will no doubt create new forms and images but it will not add anything of its own into them. The image-building faculty which was perfected by the aspirant during his earlier practices will stand him in good stead when the New Impulse directs it to communicate to the brain its instructions so that the modes of action will be vibrant with life, and will not be just soulless forms. In the priceless book *Light on the Path* it is said :

> ... in the deep silence the mysterious event will occur which will prove that the way has been found. ... The Path is found; make yourself ready to tread it.

In this silence of total negation the Third Way is found: it is in this negation that the Third Eye is opened, the eye of true spiritual insight. To tread the Path is to vitalise all modes of action and behaviour, however insignificant they may be outwardly. When the image is transformed into a symbol then one stands at the meeting point of the ascending and the descending streams of life. In the symbol the negative and the positive co-exist, and when the negative and positive exist together then is generated tremendous spiritual energy with which to vitalise one's daily life. Very often people ask : Will this silence remain? The question itself is wrong, for, the silence belongs to the realm of the Timeless. How can it be measured by the norms and standards of time ? *Light on the Path* says :

> The silence may last a moment of time, or it may last a thousand years. But it will end. Yet you will carry its strength with you.

The silence will end, for the non-dual experience comes only in moments and not in extensions of Time. But the momentary experience gives such strength that one is filled with tremendous energy to face even the fiercest battles of life. The experience of meditation can be constant but it cannot be continuous. There may be many such moments, each such experience lasting only for a moment, but it is a moment rich in eternity.

In the Symbol there takes place the mystery both of Withdrawal as well as Return. Its negation is the act of With-drawal, but the positive impulse which it receives from Above is the act of Return. In every experience of meditation, the experience where the self-image is transformed into a Symbol, there is formed an inner nucleus which gets strengthened and becomes the dynamic force for one's outer life. The nucleus has no similarity with the centre about which we discussed earlier. The centre is formed and nourished by the content of the mind. But the nucleus, vibrant with energy, is nourished by the new impulses that come from Above. The vibrating energy of the nucleus uses the symbol for the transmission of its impulses. Even the nucleus of a physical atom is not static but intensely dynamic; much more so is the Spiritual Nucleus which initiates and nourishes all outer actions and behaviour. Frithjof Schuon in his book *The Transcendental Unity of Religions* says :

> The presence of an Esoteric nucleus in a civilization guarantees to it a normal development and a maximum of stability; this nucleus, however, is not in any sense, a part even an inner part, of the Exotericism, but represents, on the contrary, a quasi-independent dimension in relation to the latter.

It is in moments of Meditation that the Inner or the Esoteric nucleus of one's life is formed and nourished. But the Esoteric is not a part, not even an inner part, of the Exoteric. The two are dimensionally different, and yet they mysteriously meet in the House of the Symbol. Without such an Esoteric nucleus the life, both of the individual and the collective, must wither. Today we see the absence of such a nucleus. There is no wonder man is broken up from within and is broken up from without too. Meditation opens the Third Eye and in this opening we are vouchsafed the vision of the Third Way.

It is the Third Way that indicates how the Exoteric life of man can be constantly energised by the Esoteric nucleus. But for this one must come to the experience of Silence, deep and profound silence — where alone the Third Way can be found. In the negation of the image, the symbol is born, and it is the symbol which initiates a moment where the Above and the Below come together, it is in the silence of the symbol that the Lover and Beloved meet. It is in the silent moments of Meditation that the Voice of the Spirit can be heard, and it is in this silence that the chrysalis is broken and the birth of the New Man takes place, a new spiritual species comes into being due to which the evolutionary stream gets a new direction for its movement. Bursting forth from the chrysalis of the past, the New Human Individual becomes the precursor of a New Age. The miraculous event happening in the silent retreat of the Symbol is indeed the fruit and the fruition of Meditation, for, it is here that the fundamental Transformation of the Human Mind takes place — an event of great spiritual import both for the human being as well as the human race. *Light on the Path* rightly says :

> Call it by what name you will, it is a Voice that speaks when there is none tospeak, it is a messenger that comes, a messenger without form or substance; or it is the flower of the soul that has opened.

SELECTED BIBLIOGRAPHY

The Secret Doctrine — H. P. Blavatsky. Synthesis of Science, Religion and Philosophy under Cosmogenesis and Anthropogenesis — Six Volumes. Theosophical Publishing House, Adyar, Madras. India

The Laws of the Higher Life — Annie Besant. Theosophical Publishing House, Adyar.

Twelve Upanishads — Theosophical Publishing House, Adyar.

The Bhagavad Gita — Annie Besant and Dr. Bhagavan Das. Theosophical Publishing House, Adyar.

Yoga Sutra of Patanjali — Yoga - the Art of Integration — Rohit Mehta. Theosophical Publishing House, Adyar.

From Mind to Super-mind — Commentary on the Bhagavad Gita by Rohit Mehta. New Order Book Co., Ahmedabad, India.

The Call of the Upanishads — Commentary on Eleven Upanishads. Bharatiya Vidya Bhavan, Bombay, India.

Vijñāna Bhairava — Kshema Raja Kashmir Sanskrit Series.

The Flight of the Eagle — J. Krishnamurti.

The Impossible Question — J. Krishnamurti.

The Urgency of Change — J. Krishnamurti.

Freedom from the Known — J. Krishnamurti.

Commentaries on Living — J. Krishnamurti (All books of J. Krishnamurti can be had from Krishnamurti Foundation, Vasanta Vihar, Greenways Road, Madras, India)

The Nameless Experience — Rohit Mehta, Motilal Banarsidass, Delhi.

Concentration and Meditation — The Buddhist Lodge, London.

Haṭha Yoga Pradīpikā — Adyar Library, Adyar.

Gheraṇḍa Samhitā — by Ma Yoga Shakti.

The Way of Mindfulness — Bhikku Soma. The Mahabodhi Society, Calcutta, India.

Tao-Teh-King—Lao Tzu — Translated by Isabella Mears. Theosophical Publishing House, London.

Gods in Exile — J. J. Van Der Leeuw. Theosophical Publishing House, Adyar.

What We shall Teach – C. Jinarajadasa. Theosophical Publishing House, Adyar,

Intelligence Came First — Edited by E. Lester Smith. Theosophical Publishing House, Wheaton, Illinois, U. S. A.

The Biology of God –– Alister Hardy. Jonathan Cape, London.

Psycho-cybernetics — Maxwell Maltz. Prentice Hall, U. S. A.

Transcendental Unity of Religion — F. Schuon. Faber and Faber, London.

Spiritual Perspectives — F. Schuon. Faber and Faber, London.

The Wisdom of Lao-tse — Lin Yutang. Michael Joseph, London.

The Tao of Physics — F. Capra, Fontana/Collins.

The Nature of Time — G. J. Whitrow, Penguin.

The Conscious Mind — Kenneth Walker.

Letters on Yoga — Sri Aurobindo.

Synthesis of Yoga — Sri Aurobindo.

Savitri — a Legend and Symbol — Sri Aurobindo (Books by Sri Aurobindo can be had from Sri Aurobindo Ashram, Pondicherry-India)

The Dialogue with Death — Rohit Mehta. S.A.B.D.A., Pondicherry-India.

The Miracle of Descent — Rohit Mehta. S.A.B.D.A., Pondicherry-India.

The Voice of the Silence — H. P. Blavatsky Theosophical Publishing House, Adyar.

Light on the Path — Mabel Collins, Theosophical Publishing House, Adyar.

Human Brain — John Pfeiffer.

Nurslings of Immortality — Dr. Raynor Johnson.

Supernature — Lyall Watson. Coronet Books, London.

The Secret of Yoga — Gopi Krishna.

Higher Consciousness — Gopi Krishna.

Kundalini — The Evolutionary Energy in Man — Gopi Krishna.

The Serpent Fire — Arthur Avalon. Ganesh & Co., Madras.

Experiment in Depth — P. W. Martin.

Man — Bridge Between Two Worlds — F. E. Winkler. Hodder and Stoughton, London.
Mind and Memory Training — E. Wood, Theosophical Publishing House, Adyar.
Talks with Ramanamaharshi — Ramana Ashrama, Tiruvannamalai, India.
Sadhana — Rabindra Nath Tagore. Macmillan & Co.
Stray Birds — Rabindra Nath Tagore, Macmillan & Co.
Thinking in Opposites — Paul Roubiczec.
Introducing Science — Alan Issacs — Penguin.